D1112617

5

Pageant
of
Life

LOWELL THOMAS, 1892-

PAGEANT OF
LIFE

PUBLISHED BY

P. F. Collier & Son Corporation, New York

BY SPECIAL ARRANGEMENT WITH

Wilfred Funk, Inc.

NEW YORK

Contents

ASSIGNMENT FROM THE CITY EDITOR   1

THE DOLLARS AND CENTS OF IT   6

SUCH IS LIFE   18

IT'S ALL IN THE FAMILY   31

THOSE DEAR LITTLE CHILDREN   42

ANIMAL INTEREST   55

RULERS OF NATIONS   83

HEADLINERS OF LIFE   123

PERSONALITIES IN ART   168

PROFESSIONALS OF PERIL   194

MISDEED AND RETRIBUTION   210

THE WONDER AND THE MARVEL   241

COMIC CONCLUSION   258

Pageant of Life

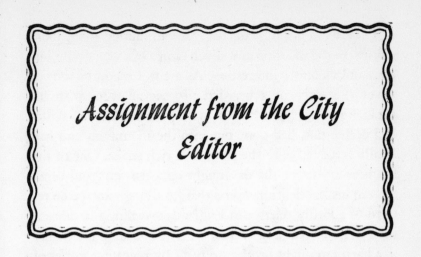

Assignment from the City Editor

*T*HERE'S an old expression, trite and threadbare from overuse. It's one of those bits of jargon that would seem to be overdue for the discard. Yet what else can you employ to signify the meaning? I refer to the familiar newspaper cliché—human interest. It is stale journalese, but tell me how to say it otherwise? So I'll speak unabashedly of human interest.

I grew up in the newspaper school of the human-interest story. Before college and then during collegiate years I was a reporter and editor in mining towns of that greatest of all western gold camps, the Cripple Creek District. I worked on dailies at Cripple Creek and Victor. It was the era when the city editor's incessant command was—human interest. The cub reporter was hounded with the insistence that human-interest stories were, more than anything else, what he was paid to get.

They were not difficult to gather in mining-town journalism. In the old gold and silver camps life was all too human and violently interesting. As a cub I might be sent to cover the story of a bearded prospector who, with his packed donkey loaded down with pick and shovel, skillet and coffee pot, had gone out into the mountains and had finally returned with the story of a rich strike. One of the headline stories of the day might concern some old-timer who in his last delirium asked that his dying message be related to a lordly relative in England, revealing that he was the black sheep of a titled family. The consumptive flunky in a barroom might break into print by revealing stories of the days when he was on the crew at Harvard. And there was the inevitable dance-hall girl who had followed the Trail of Ninety-Eight down the Yukon and was still carrying on at the Colorado camps—as frayed of looks as of morals now, yet an authentic personality of adventure in the wilds.

I graduated to big-time journalism when I got a job on a paper in Denver, and there I heard the command of the city editor in full stentorian terms: "Let's have more human interest." They developed mighty specialists in that line. I came during the Nell Brinkley, Fay King period; just after the Damon Runyan era. And what a master feature-writer Damon turned out to be! I had to compete with men far more gifted than I, including Gene Fowler, who later became a New York editor, and gained fame for his book, "Timber Line," as well as for plays for stage and screen.

Chicago next—and the old-time Midwestern metropolis

was an American Athens for the kind of story telling that concentrated on emotions and oddities of people in the news. The times were lurid and so was journalism, then as later, in Chicago. As I recall it, a full reportorial day might go something like this: Covering a Sicilian murder in Little Hell, an hour or two sitting beside Madame Schumann-Heink at her divorce trial, the task of relieving some other fellow who had been covering the Cooks and Waiters Strike, and finally ending the day by getting a story at a banquet of the Indiana Society, where you listened to story telling by Wilbur Nesbitt, George Barr McCutcheon, and George Ade.

In Chicago I trained with some of the greatest human-interest experts who ever came down the pike. My city editor was Dick Finnegan, who topped the field. For competition, there were such crack newspaper men as Floyd Gibbons, before he started storming from continent to continent, Webb Miller, who later became European head of the United Press, Marquis James, who has since won the Pulitzer Prize as a novelist, Bob Casey, who still roams the globe in Seven League Boots for the Chicago Daily News, Ben Hecht, later to make a name for himself as a writer for stage and screen, Carl Sandburg, who tells the world about Abe Lincoln, and Edgar Lee Masters of *Spoon River Anthology* fame. Give any one of these a new incident with half an emotion in it, and he'd tear hearts apart with the flip of a pen—or rather, the click of a typewriter.

Chicago completed the task of giving me a thorough grounding in the nature, value and necessity of the human-interest story. I got plenty of practice. If a vivacious daughter of a Chicago millionaire ran away with her father's jockey, I was likely to be assigned to cover the romantic event. If there wasn't time to get back to the office and write the article myself, I'd phone it in—phone it to a great re-write man, Arthur Pegler, father of Columnist Westbrook. If a story needed some master touch in the art of jerking a newspaper tear or working up a feature-story smile, Arthur Pegler was the wizard who could supply it.

My star performance as a reporter was the presentation of an astonishing affair of phoney philanthropy—the exposé of a big-hearted and lavish-handed lover of humanity who turned out to be the arch swindler of that era. The bonus I got for the assignment should really have gone to Arthur Pegler—only he didn't need the money as much as I did.

Such was the training I had for what turned out to be a career of travel and adventure and then of radio news broadcasting. And always it seemed to me that I was still hearing the well-remembered voice of the city editor: "Get the human-interest story." I did—whenever I possibly could. Today, in looking back on experiences in World War Palestine and Arabia, memory dwells on such figures as the elderly Captain Hubert Berkeley, King of Pygmy Land, who fought with Allenby in his campaign against the Turks. He was far beyond the age limit when Allenby took him out of the Front Line and put him in charge of camel transport across the blazing Sinai Desert. When I think of Lawrence of Arabia and the romantic story I got from him, I can still see the queerly anomalous figure of the Scottish doctor who turned into a dynamite enthusiast who carried T.N.T. in his stretcher and became a specialist in the blowing up of Turkish railroads.

Later, in telling the news on the radio, I paid as much heed as ever, or more, to the echo of the city editor's voice: "We must have more human interest in this paper." The recollection provided me with a number-one point of news broadcasting policy—stress the human side of the tidings of the day. Play up the boy-and-dog story, the romance of swain and sweetheart, the pathos of mother and son, the adventure of the daring individual, the alternations of tragedy and absurdity—human interest. This, I decided, was as important to a radio news program as the major events of the day—a necessary ingredient to go along with national affairs and international, with politics and war.

Having been a lifelong gatherer of stories, perhaps you can surmise the tenor of the collection I have—endless tales from everywhere. Now, from these I've made a selection, just to prove—to myself, I suppose—that I have carried out City Editor Dick Finnegan's assignment: "Get that human-interest story!"

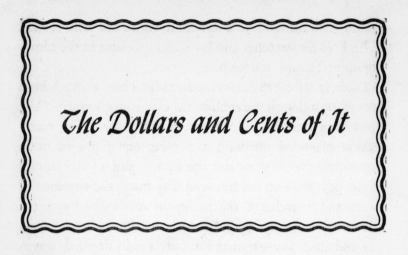

The Dollars and Cents of It

*W*HATEVER *may be the diversity of human nature,
there's no doubt about the worldwide similarity of economics. That's a theme we find everywhere in the affairs of
men—the vagaries of wealth, the ups and downs of fortune,
the business of getting a living. No nation is without the
thrill that comes from the sudden acquiring of great possessions or without the pathos of dire reversal of fortune. One
theme occurs with strange persistence—that of the ragged
wretch who stirs pity, yet who has secret wealth. The rich
miser, the capitalist mendicant. In the Pageant of Life we
find economics everywhere.*

*
=

THIS STORY MIGHT BE HEADED, "STRIKE SETTLED BY FISH Hooks." At Bridgeton, New Jersey, the pickets were parading in front of the plant of the New Jersey Packing Company. Herbert Smalley, the treasurer of the company, came out of the gate and looked at the platoon of striking workmen.

He called out with a grin, "What's the use of parading up and down like that? Why don't you fellows go home and get your tackle and come along and go fishing with me?"

At the mention of fishing, some of the pickets grinned back at him, and twenty-two of them said "Okay."

They got their rods and lines, and the treasurer took them fishing in his big motorboat. The big ones were biting, and I suppose that settled the issue. When the fishing is good it makes the heart of the fisherman glad. They caught a hundred and fifty assorted weak and blue. In between bites they told fish stories, and in between fish stories they ironed out the strike difficulties.

Back on shore the angling strikers put away their rods and reels, scaled the fish, and told the other strikers about the terms they had arranged. The next day the men were back at work.

MYNHEER JONKERS LIVED FOR EIGHTEEN YEARS IN THE greatest poverty in the Transvaal. He owned a little farm, a plot of ground from which he eked out a meager living. He put in most of his time digging, not potatoes, but diamonds, in the hope of finding the gem which would make him rich. Moralists will probably say Mynheer Jonkers would have been better off if he had busied himself with carrots rather than carats. Indeed, after eighteen years' digging, Mynheer Jonkers had just about made up his mind to do just that.

At the end of the eighteenth year he said to his wife, "Wilhelmina, it's no use."

The legend relates that his wife replied: "Jacobus, try one day more."

Jacobus did, and next day, sure enough, his pick struck a hard object which, when the dirt was cleaned off, turned out to be a diamond the size of a hen's egg, a stone without a flaw, one of the largest in the world. After it had been polished, it still weighed seven hundred and twenty-five carats.

Another legend connected with this stone is that when it was shipped to England, a formidable armed escort was sent along to guard it. But it was not the real diamond that the armed guards were protecting. The actual gem was dispatched by ordinary first-class mail. Later it was cut in New York, with great ceremony, into two million dollars' worth of diamonds.

Mynheer Jacobus Jonkers got enough out of it to make him a well-to-do man. He continued to live on the farm where he found his fortune. He spent the money on his family, and bought small farms for poor white people in

Africa, farms to enable them to support themselves while engaged in their perpetual diamond hunt.

IN NEVADA A BEWHISKERED, TATTERED BEGGAR STOPPED A business man on the street and begged for a dime for a cup of coffee. This business man took one look at the shabby tramp, and the two men recognized each other. Thirty years before, in a Nevada gold camp, a boy had stood at a gambling table and lost every nickel he had. He looked pretty sad, that kid who had played the part of a fool and his money. The gambler who operated the table was a hard old hombre of the West. I suppose he had the heavy mustaches and the checkered vest and all.

"Is that your last dollar, kid?" asked the gambler.

The boy nodded.

"How much will it take to get you back where you came from?"

The boy answered that the fare was seven dollars and fifty cents. The gambler handed him the money.

"I'll pay you back when I get home," the lad faltered.

"Never mind, kid," replied the gambler, "I don't need it. Plenty more where it came from." Which was quite true. Money was about the most plentiful thing of all in those old mining camps.

Thirty years later came the meeting of the beggar

[9]

and the business man on the street in Las Vegas, Nevada.

"I owe you seven dollars and a half," said the business man to the tramp.

A few minutes later the two men were in the best restaurant in town, and the tramp was eating the biggest meal he had had in a long time. In his pocket now was fifteen dollars, twice the sum he had given to the frightened youth of thirty years before. Moreover, he had a friend and presently a job.

IN ITALY, IN THE CITY OF MILAN, PEOPLE TALKED WITH rapturous admiration about an unknown gentleman. Ah, what a magnificent gentleman he was, so noble, so lofty of soul! Strolling along at night—dressed in his underclothing and wearing a tall silk hat.

The story relates that a group of workmen at a late task were warming themselves around a bonfire. With them was a sixty-year-old baker without a job, dressed in rags, a picture of misery. Just then along came a gentleman in evening clothes, tails and all, boiled shirt, expensive topcoat, and a shiny top hat. He saw the unemployed beggar in rags, and a surprising thing happened. The stately gentleman took off his topcoat, tailcoat, waistcoat, and boiled shirt, and gave them to the astonished poor man shivering in his rags. All the rich man retained was his underwear and his plug hat.

[10]

Clad in these, he continued on his way, shivering a little but as dignified as ever—like a modern Francis of Assisi.

In 1925 the Italian freighter, *Ignazio Florio*, was sinking in mid-Atlantic. The United States liner, *President Harding*, arrived on the scene at the eleventh hour. But the sea was too rough and the ship was in such sore distress that it was too late to think of getting a line aboard her. It was necessary for a boat's crew to volunteer to take a lifeboat over the giant waves and save the thirty-eight men aboard the Italian freighter. The first American sailor to volunteer for the arduous job was Salvatore Bracco. Well, that was fine. He got five medals and an illuminated scroll describing his heroism. He received it from the hands of Mussolini himself.

In January 1929 another Italian ship, the *Florida*, was foundering off the Virginia Capes. Along came the famous Captain Fried in the United States liner, *America*. Again there was the call for volunteers. Again the first to respond was Salvatore Bracco. Once again he got honors in abundance. New York City gave him a reception. So did his home town, Union City, New Jersey. Uncle Sam decorated him with the Congressional Medal of Honor. Italy handed out two medals and he got seven others from various American sources.

After that the world forgot Salvatore Bracco. His heart went bad on him, and it was impossible for him to go to sea any more. Ashore he could get no job. All his savings went. The people who had once cheered him paid no attention. His wife and little son were starving. He had to go on relief. For himself, his wife, his son, the one-time hero got seven and a half dollars a week. Fifteen medals and seven dollars and a half a week!

Then he died, and everybody said, "What a pity!" Union City buried him with military honors. High officials of the American Merchant Marine were in the funeral procession.

I think the bitter irony of that story is too plain to need any comment. I've always felt that the Congressional Medal of Honor should carry an income with it—as the British V.C. does. There are not many of them—holders of our most distinguished decoration.

IN ENGLAND, DEATH BROUGHT TO AN END A STRANGE AND tragic career. A disfrocked clergyman mauled by a lion succumbed to his injuries.

For years the Reverend Harold Davidson was rector in an English town spelled Stiffkey and pronounced Stewky, according to those curious ways of pronunciation in England. He had rather a sensational and brilliant career in the church. The Reverend Harold Davidson devoted himself to the rehabilitation of London's underworld, saving derelicts, preaching in the slums, a pastor of the poor. Then he became involved in a scandal, was tried on charges of immorality, and was expelled from the ministry. That was a London headline at the time.

After he was disfrocked, the former clergyman adopted a singular profession—combined lion trainer and preacher. In a circus side show he put the wild beasts through their paces and delivered a sermon. He called his act, "Davidson in the Lion's Den."

Such was his career until one day when he was going through his routine. Having led his lions through their act, he was preaching—the great cats grouped around him. In the fervor of his exhortation, he made a false step, and accidently trod on the paw of a lioness. The lioness roared, and instantly her mate, a shaggy-maned old lion, leaped upon the former rector of Stewky, hurled him down, and tore him with fang and claw. He'd have been killed instantly, save for the brave quickness of a girl performer in the side show. With a whip she drove off the angry beast, and the injured man was taken to a hospital.

The next day crowds thronged the amusement park and the side show. There big ballyhoo signs were posted. "See the lion that clawed the rector," proclaimed the advertising, and it drew the business. Meanwhile, at the hospital—the rector died.

"Cheerio, there! I say, will you have a hot dog?"

It's Lord Edward Montagu, second son of the ninth Duke of Manchester, who is speaking—selling hot dogs. His Lordship opened a hot-dog stand at the famous summer resort of Maidenhead on the Thames.

He got into the news when he announced that he was going to enlist in the French Foreign Legion and presumably seek death on the battlefield. Some declared it was because of unrequited love. But he changed his mind, changed it about death on the battlefield, and went in for hot dogs instead. Then it became evident that His Lordship was merely broke. He did quite a good business with his Oxford accent and his athletic frame, cultivated on the cricket fields. What cockney wouldn't buy a hot dog from a lord?

"Hi si, 'Arriet, 'ave a 'ot dog from 'is Lordship."

In his first day's business Lord Edward cleared a tidy profit of four pounds and two pence. "And, dash it all, that's better than the French Foreign Legion," he said.

That latest oddity was just another illustration of interesting conditions in the Dukedom of Manchester: not too much money, but plenty of original ideas—a dukedom in the shadows.

A New York policeman, Thomas Fitzpatrick, tried to arrest a beggar on the street. He chased the mendicant,

[14]

but couldn't catch him. Some while later the policeman was passing a swanky and expensive bar. He looked in rather longingly. It was a resplendent place, the kind that's a bit high-priced for a patrolman's pocketbook. He saw a man at a table, a gentleman drinking a bottle of fine wine. His face was familiar. The policeman recognized him as the beggar he had recently chased and failed to catch. A little while later the judge gave the luxurious mendicant thirty days in a not so sumptuous jail.

* =

HERE'S A STORY ABOUT ABDUL, WHO SAID HE WAS A POOR man. Abdul was a Turkish farmer of Asia Minor. He brought his son to a doctor in a near-by town.

"Allah is great," cried Abdul, "but my son is sick."

The doctor looked over the boy and said he'd have to have an X-ray made.

"Allah is merciful," chanted Abdul, "and he loves a merciful physician. How much would it cost, this thing you call X-ray?"

The doctor responded that it would cost seven dollars.

"Allah loves the true believer, but that is too much money. I am a poor man. It is more than I can pay."

The doctor, taking pity on the poverty-stricken patriarch, brought the price down to four dollars. And Abdul, still calling upon Allah and the prophet Mohammed, forked over the four bucks.

[15]

His son was afraid of the X-ray machine, and didn't want to get near the strange contraption. Abdul, in order to encourage the youth, volunteered to have the X-ray shot through him, just to show that it didn't hurt. So for the purpose of encouraging the boy, the doctor took an X-ray picture of the venerable old Turk. Right there a strange thing was observed. The X-ray didn't show that Abdul had any organic disorder. It merely revealed that he had around his waist a belt filled with gold pieces. The poverty-stricken old Moslem had two thousand dollars in gold strapped around him.

Then it was the doctor's turn to call upon Allah. "Does the prophet Mohammed command men to be liars? Does the Koran teach that you are to say you are a poor man when you have gold hidden away?"

"Allah is great," sighed old Abdul. "He is wise and He is merciful."

But, just the same, the venerable old rogue had to pay the seven dollars for the X-ray picture.

IN CHICAGO A MAN WENT AROUND SELLING MATCHES. IN HIS pocket he carried a judgment in his favor for three hundred and thirty-three thousand dollars, and he owned a seat on the Chicago Stock Exchange.

James L. Cook had been a Chicago millionaire. The crash

wiped out his fortune. He got a judgment against men who, he claimed, had tricked him out of a fortune. But he couldn't collect it. Penniless, he sold matches on the street—but still kept his seat on the Stock Exchange. He wouldn't sell it. "I might need it again, sometime," he explained.

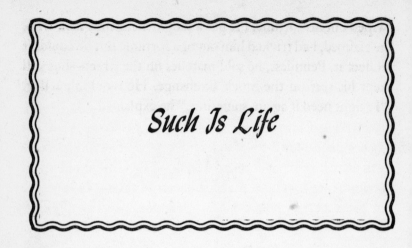

Such Is Life

FROM every place and clime come the tales that tell that human nature is always the same—or is it different? Is the old adage true—that individuals are essentially one at heart? Let's make a quick selection of stories of the largest variation, about persons of most diverse nations, and see if we can detect the identity of human nature. Is it the same old mortal man merely placed in contrast of circumstance, or does he show essential differences? These are prime questions to be posed as we contemplate the largeness of the Pageant of Life.

DON TOMÁS OF THE ARGENTINE WAS AN ENEMY OF THE flowers. He fought against blooms and blossoms. He waged war against the roses, was at strife with lilies, struggled with a mortal hate against violets, dahlias and chrysanthemums.

Tall, gaunt and stately, like a hidalgo of old, Don Tomás did not believe in saying it with flowers. He said it with words. He was a professional deliverer of eulogies, a speaker of beautiful words for the dear departed. The modern idea was that flowers at a funeral were enough. The older Argentine idea had been that the deceased should have words of great praise spoken in their memory. Hence the "official and professional eulogist," of which Don Tomás was a Ciceronian example—and the last of his tribe.

He stationed himself at the Chacarito Cemetery in Buenos Aires, and whenever a funeral entered he approached with solemn, Hispanic dignity. Tenderly he spoke words of sympathy. Benevolently he offered to make a speech at the grave, a solemn and befitting eulogy. All he needed to know was the name and profession of the dear one. With these he could make an oration of praise by the hour. He could tell of the virtues of the deceased, the grief of the family, the misfortune of the community —all in the most high-flown Spanish and embellished with Greek and Latin quotations. The cost was little, Señor. A mere pittance—one dollar for each ten minutes. Six pesos for an hour. For a eulogy of six hours there might be some slight reduction, Señor.

Of late years things had not gone so well with Don Tomás, the last of the eulogists of the Argentine. People had new ideas. They had come to think that flowers were enough, wreaths, floral pieces. They no longer thought it necessary that great words of praise should be spoken. They said it with flowers, which made business bad for Don Tomás.

That is why Don Tomás was an enemy of flowers, fought against blooms and blossoms, waged war against the roses, was at strife with lilies, struggled with a mortal hate against violets, dahlias and chrysanthemums.

He fought a losing battle—this Don Quixote tilting against the flowers. Funerals came with heaped-up floral tributes, and in vain did Don Tomás offer to pronounce his eulogies in the most high-flown Spanish with Greek and Latin phrases. It got so bad that he scarcely delivered one eulogy a month. The flowers that he loathed and despised were winning.

Then the battle came to an end. Don Tomás died and was buried. There was no eulogy at his grave. There was no eulogist left. His coffin was banked with heaps of flowers.

DOWN IN MEXICO A CURIOUS MYSTERY WAS SOLVED. A RED Communist banner had appeared on the tower of the great Cathedral of Mexico City, and nobody knew how it got there. After an investigation the police discovered that the old bell ringer had put it there. He lived in the Cathedral belfry. His father and grandfather had spent their lives taking care of the bells. He was married in the belfry. Forty-two years he lived with his bells, and then he started to brood about life and politics. He fell in with the Communists, and became a Red, so passionately proletarian that he hung out the glaring Red Communist banner from the steeple of the Cathedral. The bells were silent until they got a new bell ringer. The old one was in jail.

*
=

THERE'S MANY A STORY ABOUT THE PATIENCE OF ORIENTALS —the Japanese, for example—and a classic is to be found in the case of the postmaster of Atshushio.

For twenty-five years he was in charge of the mail at Atshushio, a town of three thousand people. And for twenty-five years the Atshushians complained about him. That was a long time, especially when you consider the offense of which the postmaster was guilty. He had a vivid curiosity about other people's affairs, and was an inveterate gossip. Being postmaster gave him his great opportunity. He steamed open every letter that passed through his hands, and read the contents—read secrets, looked over unpaid bills, and chuckled over scandal. Then he gossiped about it. He could do that all the better because he was also the local tavern keeper.

So you can see the plight of the people of Atshushio. Their hidden lives were revealed by the postmaster, as he served cups of saki in his tavern. A prominent citizen couldn't write to a geisha without having it become public. A housewife couldn't write expressing her opinion about her neighbor without everybody knowing it—including the neighbor.

The people of Atshushio wrote to Tokyo, complaining about the postmaster. For twenty-five years they kept sending complaints. But nothing ever happened. The postmaster went right along reading the mail and gossiping. But even oriental patience can become exhausted. After twenty-five years of writing complaints, the people of Atshushio finally took up a collection, and sent a delegate to the Minister of Communication in Tokyo—to present an ultimatum. They couldn't stand it any longer. Something would have to be done. The Ministry ordered an investigation, and soon Atshushio had a new postmaster— who neither opened letters nor gossiped.

PERFUMED NEWS FROM ARABIA, LAND OF FRANKINCENSE and myrrh. A man took out some insurance. What was perfumed about that? Well, he had his nose insured. Sheik Jelal Quaraishi took out a policy with a London company for two thousand pounds' worth of insurance on his nose. No doubt it was one of those curved handsome Semitic noses, though its looks were not what made it so valuable. It was the smellingest nose in the world.

This Sheik Schnozzle was a collector of rare perfumes. This Jimmy Durante of the burning sands traveled incessantly the length and breadth of Arabia, adding new rare-scented essences to his priceless collection. As the world's prime connoisseur of perfumes, the exquisitely schnozzled sheik had cultivated his sense of smell to a marvelous delicacy. Just give that ten-thousand-dollar nose of his the slightest whiff of any fragrant odor and he could analyze it for you and tell you what it was made of and how blended. It was a priceless smeller—an invaluable beezer—and it would have been a sacrilege to take a punch at a nose like that.

A STRANGE STORY CAME FROM THAT REGION OF STRANGE stories—Hollywood. A man jumped from a pier into the sea, and five life guards had a hard time rescuing him. He was Michael Romanoff, a film director of Hollywood.

Now this Mr. Michael Romanoff was, so he said, haunted by Prince Michael Romanoff. The prince was an impostor. He was said to be the son of a Cincinnati tailor, but he passed himself off as Prince Michael Romanoff, brother of the late Czar Nicholas of Russia.

He followed a profession of guile and trickery. Every

[23]

so often the report would come that somebody or other had been victimized by the bogus Prince Romanoff. And constantly, his nefarious doings were attributed to the real Michael Romanoff, the film director at Hollywood. People thought he was the one who passed himself off as a prince and talked somebody out of some money. His protests and denials were vehement, but still many people doubted.

Finally the fake prince got busy in Hollywood, and even the friends of the real Michael Romanoff grew doubtful. So the persecuted film director, haunted to desperation, jumped into the sea and had to be fished out.

IN BUDAPEST, WHERE THE HUNGARIANS ARE A HOT-HEADED race, a patient was brought to a hospital. Two doctors examined her and got into an argument—to operate or not to operate. One said "yes," the other said "no." They couldn't come to an agreement. The doctor in favor of the operation went ahead with his surgery.

A few days later he was telling about it to some other medicos, telling them how he had disagreed with his colleague, and how said colleague had been all wrong. Just then the other doctor appeared on the scene. "You shouldn't have operated," he shouted. "You look upon your patients as cases, not human beings. You operated because you're

—a 'searcher.' You wanted to see what was inside, so you could talk and write about it." The argument waxed hot and heavy. A blow was struck.

The next day the two doctors appeared on the dueling field, and operated on each other—with sabers. With heavy cavalry blades they slashed away. There were seven exchanges of cut and thrust. Both doctors were bleeding—incisions and lacerations. Then, with a sweeping blow, one nearly scalped the other. Then they shook hands. Honor was satisfied.

The operation? Oh, it was a success.

THE DOCTORS DECLARED THAT THEY COULD HAVE SAVED THE life of Alfred Grouard, if she had let them. Yes, the name was "Alfred," and the pronoun was "she." Another one of those strange cases of a woman masquerading as a man—this time tragic.

Fourteen years previously, in the home of a rich Long Island family came a new butler—short, dark-haired, quiet, soft-spoken. As the years went by, Alfred Grouard made a local reputation as the perfect butler. He had a fine character too—he passed his spare time praying and reading the Bible.

Then Alfred Grouard fell ill. His employers called a doctor. But the butler refused to be examined by the physician. For once the perfect servant was not so perfect, shrieking wild protests. His employers let him have his way. Then his condition grew serious. He tried to bear up under it, tried to deny his illness, but couldn't. Once more they called a doctor, and once more the butler revolted—with screaming hysterics. He had a weird phobia against physicians—and so he died.

Then only was it discovered that Alfred Grouard, the supreme butler, had really been a woman. The doctors found she had diabetes, and said they could easily have saved her life if she had submitted to treatment. The woman who had lived as a man had kept her disguise right on through the door of death.

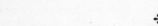

AT LOS ANGELES A COURT OF LAW WAS ASKED TO HAND down a decision in an amazing case—a freak of nature, a fantastic transformation of a human being. Edward Price Richards, twenty-nine years old and registered for the draft, petitioned the court to declare him legally a woman—because he had turned into one. He stated that recently he had undergone a singular change—from one sex to another. So he asked the right to wear women's clothing and have his name changed from Edward to Barbara Ann.

In his plea to the court he said that as a boy he was normal —though rather sickly. He grew to manhood, and noticed no change until he was twenty-seven. Then things proceeded to happen. "About two years ago," he related, "I realized that some physiological change was taking place. I used to have such a heavy beard that I had to shave twice a day. Now it has stopped growing. I haven't shaved for six weeks," he added. He said the shape of his face changed and his skin became smoother and finer. His voice rose in pitch, became a contralto. "I changed to a woman mentally, too," he continued. "I wanted to stay around the house. I became fond of cooking and household duties," said he. Or was it—she? The question of pronouns was a puzzler. Edward—or Barbara Ann—appeared in court wearing a smart gown, a modish hat, lipstick and rouge.

An astonishing case—and what could have been the cause? What could have been the reason for the remarkable transformation? A Los Angeles physician stated that such a metamorphosis was quite possible, and might have been caused by illness. What kind of illness? The doctor said—the mumps, for example. That's a good old-fashioned malady—the mumps. Many of us have had them, and never dreamed of the possibilities. So, look out, boys, look out for the mumps.

A MAN LIVED AS A FOREST HERMIT IN GREATER NEW YORK —in the thick woods on Staten Island. There still are such things as woods on Staten Island, a borough of New York City. For shelter he had a pup tent. He did his own cooking,

mended and sewed his clothes on a portable sewing machine, did his own laundry in a running stream near by. He
had a radio, a complete supply of food, plenty of wearing
apparel—also a dentist's outfit. That's what got him into
trouble.

A dentist practicing in a town near by reported to the
police that his office had been broken into and some of his
most modern instruments and materials stolen. Clues took
the detectives to the hermit's lair in the thick woods of New
York City, and the anchorite confessed the burglary of
the dentist's office. He had stolen the dental instruments to
fill a couple of his own teeth, extract others, and make some
false ones. He had even taken a hypodermic set to give himself a local anesthetic.

ALL NEWSPAPER READERS KNOW THAT FAMILIAR JOURNAL-
istic section, "Letters to the Editor." If you enjoy those
communications from constant readers you may have noticed the name of Charlie ·Hopper. He was the world's
champion for writing letters to the editor. He wrote more
than seventy thousand to newspapers all over the nation.
But perhaps you never knew that Charlie Hopper was a
hermit, an anchorite of the West, living in a lonely cottage
in the wilderness of Coeur d'Alene, Idaho.

In the course of time the letter-writing champ returned

to New York, the big town he had left twenty-three years previously, when he fled into exile. Again he was seeing the metropolitan sights from which he had departed in shame and horror to become a hermit in an Idaho solitude, amid the Coeur d'Alene Mountains. In New York he went looking for something sacred to him—a thing that evoked bitter memories, a drinking fountain.

Back in 1894, Charlie's uncle, John Hopper, gave to the City of New York a drinking fountain to provide copious pure water for quenching human thirst. Nineteen years later, in 1913, nephew Charlie happened to pass the fountain. He looked and saw it was dry. Not a drop of water flowing from it, not a touch of moisture! The city had neglected the fountain, and it was as dry as the Sahara Desert. Near by, Charlie saw a beer saloon. The only place where a thirsty mortal could get a drink in that neighborhood was not at the fountain, but in the saloon. Not water, but beer.

He wrote a letter to the editor—his first. And he determined to abandon the wicked city, where there was no water, only beer. Because of the fountain he fled far away to a hermitage in Idaho. There he kept on writing letters to the editor, an endless stream. An average of thirty-one hundred a year for twenty-three years, on all subjects interesting to a philosopher. His last before returning to New York was a "Constant Reader" communication printed in the New York *Times*, a dissertation on walking and goosestepping.

But why did Charlie return? It was because he had a

mother. To be sure, Mrs. Hopper was never in doubt about Charlie's whereabouts. She never had to sigh, "Where is my wandering boy tonight?" It would be cynical to say that the writer of seventy thousand letters to the editor never wrote to his mother. Wicked cynicism, that. For Charlie wrote to his mother as copiously as he wrote to editors. She was deluged with letters. And finally Charlie returned home on Thanksgiving.

He went sight-seeing in Manhattan, and of course he made a trip to that well-remembered fountain. The news wasn't clear, but I suppose the fountain was still dry. I know there's plenty of beer in that neighborhood, and Charlie no doubt wrote another letter to the editor.

It's All in the Family

*B*LOOD *relationship is a basic element in the pageant of that kind of life which endures because parents have children and may have more than one. Father, mother, son, daughter, brother, sister—these are the figures on the stage in many a drama alight with joy or exceptional in pity and pathos. There's the sacrifice made to kindred, the quest for lost relatives, and the joys and wrangles of family life. In stories that tell of blood relationship we can find some of the most poignant of all—and some odd ones too.*

AT LOS ANGELES LIVED AN AGED WOMAN, FEEBLE, HALF blind. A daughter of hers succumbed to illness, died. Should they tell the mother, break the news to her? That may seem to have been a strange question—until we know the identity of the aged woman.

She was Mrs. Nicholas Colombo, mother of Russ Colombo, the brilliant radio and motion-picture star who six years previously had been killed in an accident with a gun. At that time the mother was ill, so ill the doctors said she would never survive the shock of the death of her son. So she was never told of Russ Colombo's untimely end. The family kept up a fiction that he was alive—was away, kept busy by his radio and motion-picture jobs and unable to get home. He could only write to her: she got letters from him regularly. Others of the family wrote the letters, supposedly from Russ Colombo to his mother; they sent one every week. That strange fiction has continued for six years.

Then a daughter died. So you see the question. Should they create a deception in the case of the daughter too? Pretend that she also was still alive? That might seem to be too much in the drama of a mother's illusion. The problem was considered for two days, and then the doctors gave a verdict. They said that the mother was now well enough to receive the news of her daughter's death, well enough to stand the shock.

But what of Russ Colombo? That was something else. They would not break to her that sad six-year-old news. Russ Colombo would still remain alive—so far as his mother was concerned. She would retain the illusion. Her remaining children continued to send her the weekly letter supposedly from him. The deception would continue as long as she lives.

*
=

Mrs. Carmella Giamusso did not understand English. Mrs. Giamusso lived in Brooklyn, and had a son. He was away from home, had been for some time, but he wrote to his mother at regular intervals. Mrs. Giamusso said her boy was a good son. Presently he wrote to her that he had moved to Atlanta, Georgia, and was in business down there. She sent a letter to the post office box he gave, and then decided to pay her boy a surprise visit. She took a train to Atlanta, went to the post office, and through an interpreter asked where she could find her son.

The clerks looked at each other.

"He's a good boy," she said. "He must have a fine business in this fine city. He will be glad to see his mother."

The post office clerks didn't know what to say, but as Mrs. Giamusso was growing impatient, they had to tell her.

And so the mother found that her son lived in a big castle with high strong walls, spacious courtyards, and many men on guard. It was a magnificent-looking castle run by the Government of the United States. Mrs. Giamusso's son was in there—for not paying sufficient heed to one of the amendments of the Constitution of the United States, the one pertaining to alcoholic beverages.

Mrs. Giamusso's face grew sad when she finally under-

[33]

stood, but she looked the post office folks straight in the eye and told them that she was going to see her son anyway. Because, even if he did live in that big castle, he was a good son just the same.

The men in the post office couldn't help thinking about various things, about their own mothers, maybe. So they got together and made a few arrangements. As Mrs. Giamusso had no money, they raised a purse, paid her hotel bill for three days' stay in Atlanta, and arranged things so she could spend most of the time with her son, in whom she had not lost faith.

*
=

THE FUNEREAL COLOR OF BLACK WAS SEEN AT A CASTLE IN France, a medieval stronghold built by the Knights Templar. Suzanne Valadon had died. She had been an artist of note. Her son was an artist of greater note. There was a strange tale of mother love.

In the old days of the Latin Quarter, when many a great name flourished in art, there was a model of singular grace and beauty—Suzanne Valadon. She posed for great masters. They taught her how to paint. Suzanne had a child, a son. Later on, the Spanish artist, Utrillo, fell in love with her, married her, and gave the boy his name, Maurice Utrillo. She taught her son how to paint. He displayed a vivid turn of genius—as an impressionist, moody and exotic. He also displayed a weakness—alcoholic.

He became a slave of tavern keepers, who would ply him with brandy, lock him in a back room, and make him pay his bills by painting pictures for them. The paintings that Utrillo produced in that fashion sold for thousands of dollars. His own mentality was gone, sinking into shadow. His mother rescued him, took him from his evil haunts.

By this time the mind of Maurice Utrillo had gone so far that he passed his time playing with children's toys. Suzanne Valadon took him away from Paris, to the country, to the medieval castle of the Knights Templar. There she fitted out one turret as a studio for herself, the other as a studio for her son. In one she painted. In the other she brought him back to health and painting—quiet years of mother love and art. And Maurice Utrillo painted in such style that the French Government decorated him with the Legion of Honor.

So you can fathom the depth of grief at the castle of the Templars over the death of Suzanne Valadon.

IN MEXICO CITY A WOMAN DIED. SHE WAS A WOMAN OF mystery. They called her La Coronela. In Spanish that's feminine for colonel. She was a colonel, the only woman ever to hold the rank of officer in the Mexican Army. She died of a broken heart.

During a Mexican revolution a woman enlisted in one of

[35]

the armies. In one battle after another she fought like a tigress. She became an officer, and was called La Coronela. She was very beautiful. Nobody knew anything about her. The soldiers said that she smiled at death and laughed at love. At the end of the revolution she had a good supply of looted gold, and disappeared, no one knew where.

Years later she reappeared in Mexico City, still beautiful, but worn and ragged. Every day she went to a little restaurant where she would sit smoking cigarettes for hours. She was there when, as they say, her heart broke. A richly dressed, beautiful girl passed by. La Coronela looked at her. The girl ignored the older woman, and walked on. La Coronela turned to a man near by, and said: "She snubbed me. Do you know who she is? She is my daughter." La Coronela's head dropped to the table.

When they went to her she was dead.

A STORY OF THE HEROISM AND FORTITUDE OF A SEVENTEEN-year-old girl came from Meanford, Ontario. June Mottershaw was in a hospital with a bullet hole through her chest. She came to the hospital after suffering from that dangerous wound for two days—and saying nothing to anybody about it.

June shot herself accidentally with a thirty-two caliber revolver. The bullet pierced the base of her left lung, just below the heart. Nobody saw the mishap, and June was afraid to tell anybody about it—afraid to go to a doctor. She thought her parents would not be able to pay the doctor bill. They were poor, and she didn't want to cause them so much expense. Injured in so perilous a way, she went about as if nothing had happened. She ate at mealtime, slept at night, answered the door bell, and talked to various friends. That—for two days.

Finally she couldn't keep the secret any longer, and mentioned to a girl friend how she had shot herself. Not that June was weakening about it—apparently she just couldn't keep a secret. Taken to a hospital, the doctor said the bullet wound might easily have been fatal, but they found no infection—and June got well.

In New York a seventeen-year-old girl was arrested, put in jail—because of her love for beauty. She loved it so much that she set the house on fire.

Mildred was a prize pupil in a Brooklyn high school on the subject of home-making—the house beautiful. The right colors for the walls, the curtains and sofa pillows, harmonious furniture to soothe the sensitive soul. But when Mildred went home, what did she see? It was awful. The taste her parents displayed in the way of chairs and tables, colors and wallpaper was something atrocious. The chandelier didn't match the picture frames. The flowers didn't match the tablecloth. It was definitely not the house beautiful, as described in the high-school course in interior decorating.

So Home Sweet Home jangled on the nerves of modern Mildred, depressed her, made her stamp her foot and grit her teeth. She tried to persuade Ma and Pa to change the furniture, get something smart and esthetic—with just a touch of modernism, perhaps. But they wouldn't do it. Ma and Pa thought the five-and-ten dishes and the plush sofa were quite okay. So what did our Millie do? She set the house on fire.

Later, in tears, she told the police how before going to school she touched a match to two mattresses in the bedrooms—the bedspreads had always been a fright. Her idea was that by burning up the household furniture, she would make Ma and Pa get something new—more in the line of beauty. The fire department wasn't enthusiastic about the idea. The smoke-eaters ate a lot of smoke in putting out the flames. It was all very tragic for Mildred—especially as the furnishings of the jail cell in which she passed some hours were not so beautiful either.

WILLIAM WYSONG AND MRS. JAMES BUCY OF INDIANAPOLIS had known each other for years. She was much older than he, and regarded him almost as a son. Then she discovered that he *was* her son! Wysong had been adopted by another family when he was a child. His mother had married again and lost track of him. Years later, by pure accident, they drifted together and finally discovered that they were mother and son.

A STREET FIGHT WAS GOING ON IN PORTSMOUTH, ENGLAND. Three men were all merrily socking away at a fourth. Old John Perett, a good Samaritan, came strolling along, and went to the aid of the underdog. He was getting the worst of it when a brawny young sailor jumped in to help him. That evened things up and made it three against three. After the rumpus was over, Old John Perett discovered that the sailor lad's name was Perett also. He turned out to be Old John's son. Twenty-five years before, Old John Perett was at sea when his wife gave birth to a boy. The mother died soon afterward, and John Perett never saw his son. That is, he never did until the brawny young sailor jumped in to help him in the street fight.

AT GUTHRIE, OKLAHOMA, TWO MEN WERE SITTING ON A bench in front of a railway station, waiting for a train. One

[39]

man reached into a bag and took out an apple. The aroma of the apple attracted the attention of the other man.

"It smells like a North Carolina apple," he remarked.

"It is," responded the chap with the apple. "I've brought these with me all the way from old North Carolina."

"Well, I'm from those parts myself," was the response. He named the North Carolina county where he came from, and it turned out that the two men were both from that county.

"My name's McBride," said one.

"And so's mine," replied the other.

As they continued to compare notes they found that they were brothers. They had drifted apart thirty years before, and had not seen each other again, until they sat down on a bench at the Oklahoma railway station and the attention of one was attracted by the aroma of the North Carolina apple.

A DAMON AND PYTHIAS STORY CAME TO ME FROM ITALY —a tale of two friends like brothers. One of them was an American, and he was being prosecuted in the Italian courts. They called him "The Knight." His name was Patrick Sullivan. He was an Irish-American artist from Boston, who had been living for twenty-two years in the village of Asolo in the Venetian Alps.

During the World War Patrick Sullivan enlisted in the

Italian Army and distinguished himself. Likewise, in the little town where he lived he had a great reputation for generous benevolences. As a result, Patrick Sullivan was knighted by the King of Italy. So they called him "The Knight."

The Damon and Pythias story began when "The Knight" was driving along a country road with Count Giuseppe Samartini of Venice. The two were great friends. The Count was at the wheel when, through no fault of his own, he struck a boy, and the injuries to the boy were fatal.

It happened that the Countess Samartini was dangerously ill, and Patrick Sullivan was afraid that, if the news of her husband's predicament got to her, it might endanger her life. So he took the blame for the accident on himself. He was held responsible and was to be tried for the mishap.

Presently the Countess recovered, and Samartini went to the rescue of his generous friend. He denounced himself as being responsible for the accident. That caused a considerable hubbub in Italian legal circles. The case ended with two prosecutions. The Count was prosecuted for the accident and Patrick Sullivan, "The Knight," was indicted for willful misrepresentation in court and false confession of guilt.

A decision was rendered as follows: The judge acquitted the Count because the accident was unavoidable. He also set Patrick Sullivan free, declaring that the legal offense was more than compensated by the magnanimous and self-sacrificing display of friendship.

Those Dear Little Children

*K*ID *stories are supposed to be cute, and often are. Yet the charm of childhood can sometimes be of a good deal less than perfect sweetness. It has long been advertised how Angel Face can be the very devil of a pesky brat. The mischief of the urchin is proverbial as an evocation of a laugh or a growl. Then, mingled with this all, is the pathos of childhood. No other theme quite equals it as good cause for the moist eye and the sentimental sigh. Very special is the Pageant of Life when it turns to pictures of the small and young.*

A SMALL BOY WALKED THROUGH THE FRONT DOOR OF THE City Hospital in Boston. He was a sturdy little five-year-old, and in his hand he had a bright red apple. Solemnly he walked up to the desk and asked for Santa Claus. The hospital people wanted to know what made him think Santa Claus was there. And the little lad explained that Mommie had said Santa was sick this year—so he had brought Santa an apple to make him well.

Later on, the hospital folks learned that the small boy's pretty young mama was a singer out of a job, no money for Yuletide, about penniless. She had told little Ronnie that the Saint of Christmas was ill, so Ronnie would understand why Kriss Kringle and his reindeer failed to come to their house.

ORDINARILY IT ISN'T EITHER AMUSING OR DIGNIFIED TO have a small boy throw snowballs at you. I can speak from past experience and several dented derbys. But here's a case that was different.

At New Britain, Connecticut, Orazio Puglisi, driving along in his automobile, was horrified to see a boy take a slide on the slippery roadway and land right in front of the swift-moving car. He jammed on his brakes with a convulsive bit of rapid action. The car did a dizzy skid—and there was the boy hanging onto the front bumper of the machine. The lad had made a quick and skillful grab as the car had borne down on him.

Was the boy hurt? Well, his feelings were badly hurt.

He was mad as a hornet. He ran to a near-by snowbank and started firing snowballs at the man in the car. So that's how it happened that one chap at least was tickled to death when a small boy started snowballing him.

*
=

AT ECHO LAKE, IN THE MOUNTAINS OF NORTHERN NEW Jersey, a three-hour gun battle was fought. A posse of police officers besieged a cabin in the rugged country—mountain vacation ground in the summer, but a deserted wilderness in the winter. From the cabin came an incessant fusillade—rifle and shotgun. To this the police replied from behind trees and boulders. They fought cautiously—for the desperate resistance from the besieged cabin seemed to indicate outlaws of the most desperate sort. With wary strategy the forces of the law crept closer, narrowing the circle.

After three hours of this skirmishing and shooting, a state trooper was able to get to a window of the cabin—and into it he tossed a tear-gas bomb. That's usually the deciding trick against besieged desperadoes. There's no resisting the lachrymose vapor which blinds the eyes with burning tears. So the posse waited for the gunmen to emerge. They were not disappointed, but were they surprised!

Out of the cabin, with dirty faces and red eyes, came two small boys. Fourteen-year-old lads, each about four-

feet-two in height. Thus ended the battle of Echo Lake—
the desperadoes turning out to be a couple of runaway kids.
Formidable juveniles, for in the cabin the police found five
twenty-two caliber rifles, a double-barreled shotgun, a
single-barreled shotgun, five hundred rounds of ammunition, eight hunting knives, a hatchet, and an army bayonet!

The two lads had run away from home, stolen a milk
truck, driven it for some miles, and then abandoned it.
They stole three automobiles in rapid succession, one a
policeman's. Transferring from one stolen car to another,
they got to the Echo Lake section, and proceeded to break
into cottages and cabins. They specialized in taking guns
and other weapons, and even got an army bayonet.

The police got word of prowlers around the summer
places, and the trail led to the cabin in the hills. As they
approached they were greeted by a volley of shots—and
the battle of Echo Lake was on.

The lads, taken back to their home town of Paterson,
told the prosecutor that they had planned a hunting trip,
were going out to the mountains to shoot deer. Their hunting trip turned into what was something like a war.

A BUS IN BROOKLYN WAS RUMBLING ALONG AN AVENUE,
when down the line the driver saw two children on tricycles
—a ten-year-old boy and a seven-year-old girl pedaling

along. There was something about them that attracted the bus driver's attention—they were riding their tricycles with so much earnestness and industry. He stopped and asked them where they were going.

"We're going to California," said the boy.

That astonished the Brooklyn busman no little. "Hop in," said he, "and I'll give you a lift—on your way to California."

He drove the children around to the nearest police station, and there the cops questioned them. The ten-year-old boy, dark and rather stern, wouldn't say much. He merely frowned. The seven-year-old girl, with stringy blond hair and a freckled nose, was less reserved. The boy's name was Armand Mascato, she said. And hers Janet Every. They lived in the same Brooklyn house, and at dawn that morning, four A. M., Armand had crept to her bed.

"He woke me up," she related, "and said we had to travel."

They packed their clothes, and started out. They had two tricycles, which they had found the day before in a vacant lot. They were on the way to the home of a relative of Janet's when they decided they'd go to Coney Island, and finally, they figured, to California—why not? On their tricycles they pedaled for two miles—before the bus driver picked them up.

The police phoned an inquiry to the Children's Aid Society, and there the reply was prompt. The boy was an orphan. The girl's father was dead. They had been given to the custody of the Children's Aid Society, which in turn had placed them to live in the home of Mrs. Edith Hall in Brooklyn. That morning, Mrs. Hall, getting up at a reasonable time, missed the two and had informed the Society. It would appear that the ten-year-old and the seven-year-old had an attack of wanderlust—probably because they happened to find two tricycles.

AT WILMINGTON, NORTH CAROLINA, THERE WAS A YOUNGSTER who certainly had a talent for business. He made a neat bit of profit by selling measles. Yes, the old familiar rash called measles.

He had the measles himself and was delighted to find that it kept him out of school. He got word to some other boys and suggested that they also could dodge school by getting the measles. In fact, he'd sell the measles to them. He would let them sneak up to his room, unobserved and they could sit there long enough to get a case of red-rash measles for themselves. He would only charge them ten cents apiece. Seven schoolboys fell for the proposition. They paid their ten cents and got their measles. That made a net profit of seventy cents for the smart boy. His cleverness resulted in a small epidemic of measles at Wilmington.

At Bayonne, New Jersey, they found Jimmy O'Connell—after a wide and anxious search. Jimmy's father was a policeman, and so his brother cops made extra efforts to find the ten-year-old lad. There was poignant worry, because Jimmy had last been seen out on the ice of Newark Bay—floating ice. It was feared he had been swept away by the tide.

Next day they found Jimmy—in the basement of his home, hiding there. During all the hunt for him he had been hiding. Why? What was it all about? It took a little time to get it out of the lad. Jimmy had indeed been out on the ice, skipping from one ice floe to another. Then he started home and saw the cops hunting for him. Even though Jimmy's father was a policeman, Jimmy was afraid of cops—the way most boys are. They didn't see him, and he ducked into the hallway of an apartment house and fell asleep there. When he awakened he went home, and being more scared than ever, hid in the basement. There his father found him.

"Down with dancing! Down with tobacco! Down with cards! Down with all those practices of the devil!" So said the still small voice. In this case it wasn't so very still, but it was small enough—five years old. It emanated from Kansas City, Missouri, where the youngest evangelist in the world was holding forth, striking mighty blows against what he called the "sly old fox"—the devil.

He had been preaching ever since he was two. His father, who was a preacher, taught him. The first words he learned to lisp were evangelizing words. So now he was the Reverend Charles E. Jaynes, Jr., aged five. A disciple of Sister Aimee Semple MacPherson, of the Four Square Gospel. I suppose you'd call his a Five Year Old Gospel.

The Reverend Jaynes vociferously denounced dancing. At the age of five, he didn't dance. He excoriated tobacco. At the age of five he didn't smoke. The same thing went for cards—he didn't play poker. As for liquor—in all his five years he had never stood at the bar, hoisted a cocktail, tippled a highball or blown the suds off a glass of beer. So down with sin, at the age of Five!

Now is the time for all good men to sing a mammy song—for this is a story about Aunt Leah Williams of Fayetteville, North Carolina. She was a hundred and ten times a mammy. Eighty-five years old, and one hundred and ten children. They were not all hers, really—I mean in the usual way. You know, the strictly maternal sense. For many a year she gathered around her every Negro child, orphan, waif and stray that came her way. Sometimes she had as many as twenty at once living in her cabin. She had only a couple of chairs, so at dinner time they just stood crowded around the table while she dished out sow-belly, hoe-cake and hominy grits.

Aunt Leah had a lot of children of her own, but they were so mixed in with the crowd that she hardly knew which.

"Dey's all my chillun," she explained.

This champion mammy extended her bountiful charity even to dogs. Any stray pooch that came to her cabin was sure to get something to eat.

DURING AN EVACUATION OF CHILDREN FROM LONDON, under the bombs, one batch of tiny kiddies was sent to a sleepy village in Herefordshire. Two of them were black, a boy and a girl, very black and very small. The billeting officer, a local villager, placed the various children here and there to live in rural homes. But the country people, simple and rustic, looked with astonishment and misgiving at the two little Negroes. The billeting officer found no home in which he could place them.

He had them on his hands, and all he could do was take them to his own house. There his wife looked at the tiny black boy and girl, and was kindly and sympathetic—rather charmed by the two little blacks. She said she'd keep them.

That night, when she undressed the girl, she found pinned to her petticoat an envelope. On the envelope was written, "To the woman who undresses my babies tonight, with thanks for looking after them. God bless you." She opened the envelope and in it found Fifty Pounds—Two Hundred Dollars, a veritable fortune in a sleepy village like the one in Herefordshire.

A WOMAN FROM ENGLAND TOLD WHAT HAPPENED TO HER and her fourteen-months-old baby in one of Hitler's raids on London. For long nights she had been unable to sleep in the stuffy underground air-raid shelter. Finally came a night when she was too exhausted to go to the shelter, and she dozed off in her own house. A bomb hit the house, crashed through the roof. The bed she was sleeping in collapsed, and the walls were shaking back and forth.

She looked up through the hole that the bomb had made in the ceiling, and saw another bomb falling through the identical hole. It fell just beside the crib in which that fourteen-months-old baby was sleeping, and exploded. It blew the baby up into the air through the hole in the ceiling. The mother was hurled in such fashion that, with her arms extended, she managed to catch her baby as he fell back through the bomb hole. Miraculous as it may seem, both the baby and the mother were unharmed.

*
=

THE STAVISKY CASE WAS FLARING IN FRANCE, WHEN ONE day its grand political aspects faded away—with the story of how a woman was taken from a prison cell to a private hospital and allowed to pass an hour in a hospital bed. They bandaged her foot, and that may have seemed a crazy thing to do. Because there was nothing wrong with her foot. Yet they wrapped it in a great bundling of white. Then two children came to see her.

The two most pathetic figures in the spectacular banking scandal which shook France were a little boy and a little girl—children of Stavisky, who died a suicide. The girl, who was the older, had got her first glimpse of her father through prison bars. He had been in trouble with the law at that previous time. In fact, the child was born while he was in prison. The mother took the baby to see him in his cell. Little Arlette Stavisky was only six months old at that time, and she didn't know—didn't know about the grim stone walls and the cage-like cell.

The children were eight and seven when their father's final catastrophe came. They were not told how he died. They thought he was alive. They were told that he was on a trip to the United States.

[52]

Then the day came when their mother was arrested, charged with complicity in her husband's swindles. They didn't know that either, weren't told.

"She is ill. She is in the hospital. She hurt her foot." That was the explanation given, and they believed it. No one had the heart to tell them that their mother was in prison.

The children kept calling for their mother, and she kept calling for them. The French authorities had a way of doing fine, charming, human things. They allowed mother and children to meet, and conspired with her to keep up the illusion.

For an hour in the hospital room they were together, sad and happy—the mother sad for many a tragic reason, the children sad because of that big white bandage.

You could hear them exclaim: "Poor Mama's foot!"

IN TOKYO AN OLD RETIRED ARMY OFFICER, A MAJOR GENERAL, went to school—to grammar school, along with the boys and girls. Day after day the venerable warrior attended classes. Why? He was taking the place of his son. His boy was ill and had to be kept out of school, so the father went to school instead. He studied faithfully and hard, and each day took home what he had learned and taught it to the boy. With that devoted coaching, the lad kept up with his classes.

"As I am retired from military service," the father explained, "it's my duty to train my son to the best of my ability for the sake of our country."

*
=

IN OKLAHOMA THEY CAPTURED THE MYSTERY MAN OF THE burning books. His habit was to go into isolated rural schoolhouses at night, and in the schoolroom stove he'd burn a dozen or so textbooks. A lot of school children can sympathize. I can remember when I wanted to burn the arithmetic and make a bonfire of the spelling and grammar. In Oklahoma this weird sort of vandalism happened time after time. So a manhunt was staged, the Oklahoma way—with bloodhounds. The hounds caught up with the mysterious burner of books. He turned out to be a roving vagrant, wandering around among the hills. "I've been living mostly on raisins and berries," he told the sheriff, and then added: "I'm roaming around like this because I like it."

He also liked to keep warm those frosty nights. So he'd break into a rural schoolhouse and start a fire in the stove. The handiest fuel was—the books the children studied. He'd warm up, sleep in the schoolroom, and at daybreak he'd go roaming again. The burner of school books, hero of the children of the Southwest!

Animal Interest

HUMAN society consists in part—and in an important part—of creatures that are not human at all. That is, man's attitude toward animals is part of his emotional being and is of social consequence. Consider our affection for pets, our regard for the beasts that serve us—not forgetting the laughter, curiosity, wonder, fear and odium called forth by forms of life that we call lower. The snake, the monkey, the billy goat, the nightingale, not to forget that enemy of the nose, the polecat. Human interest is also animal interest.

IT HAPPENED IN HUDSON, MICHIGAN, WHEN LIGHTNING SET fire to a farmer's barn. In the barn were twenty-five cows, and Farmer Frank Brown thought of them instantly when he saw the outbreak of flame. However, in order to save the barn, he'd have to go for help quickly. No time to drive the cattle out. It was a dilemma, but Farmer Brown solved it. He whistled for his collie dog, Scotty, and, when Scotty came bounding to his side, he said: "Go in there and drive out those cows!" He was ordering the dog into the blazing barn.

Then the farmer ran for help, but help failed him in the emergency—that is, human help. When he returned, he found the barn a smoking ruin. But there, in the adjoining pasture, were the cows—all twenty-five of them —and Scotty was keeping them together.

IN NEW YORK, ENGINE COMPANY NUMBER TWO HUNDRED and Three was in mourning for Nig. He was the victim of a hit-and-run driver; Nig, the small mongrel pooch who for ten years had been the firehouse dog. Every time the alarm sounded for Engine Number Two Hundred and Three, Nig would come scampering and take one high jump all the way up to the tall seat of the driver. Nig always made it at a single bound.

At the fire Nig would take an active part, dashing in among smoke and flames, and sometimes he saved lives. He was decorated with three life-saving medals and once received a dog magazine diploma of honor for valor. The exploit which most endeared him to the firemen was this: Nig hated cats, had an acute dislike for them. He was always chasing cats. But in a tenement-house fire Nig dashed into the blaze and saved a cat. He knew his duty, and he came out dragging a badly singed Kitty.

The firemen told the story of Nig's end. Hit by a car and badly injured, he dragged himself into the station house. He crawled to Engine Number Two Hundred and Three. Fatally hurt, he crouched and gathered all his strength and took a leap for the driver's seat, the leap he had so often made. For the first time he fell short, couldn't make it. He dropped back to the pavement and died—the end of Nig the hero dog.

YOU HEAR A LOT ABOUT HOW FAITHFUL A DOG CAN BE TO his master. But here is a story from down in Gladstone, Virginia, about a coon dog named Red. Every day for a week he was seen carrying food off down the road. Finally his master followed him to a stone quarry. There he found a collie dog named Pete that had fallen into a hole forty feet deep. Every day Red, the coon dog, had been bringing food and dropping it into the pit.

IN SYRACUSE, NEW YORK, LIVED A DOG THAT HAD BEWILDering gifts. He was a police dog named Lightning. They caught Lightning roaming the streets without a license tag, and put him in the pound of the Society for the Prevention of Cruelty to Animals. They locked him with a dozen others of his kind in a cell.

Lightning's talent was this. In the middle of the night he decided he'd had enough of that cell, so he placed his front paws on the doorknob, twisted it around, pushed open the door, and stepped out. Naturally his twelve cellmates whooped with delight and followed him. Lightning was not content with this. He went to every other cell block, and one by one he opened all six doors. The upshot of it was that Lightning set no less than forty dogs free. It was the first and only wholesale jail delivery in the history of the Syracuse S.P.C.A.—maybe in all dog history.

But that wasn't all. Lightning got into the larder. Some friend of animals had just sent over a present of sixty pounds of fresh venison, and did those dogs enjoy that venison! Lightning's talents were at their most brilliant when he opened that larder door. In order to do this he had not only to lift the bolt but to turn the knob at the same time.

When Lightning's owner came along to claim his dog and pay his fine, he remarked mildly: "Lightning is pretty good at picking locks and opening doors."

To which S.P.C.A. Director Cassidy replied: "Pretty good? He's the world's champion! But who's going to replace that sixty pounds of venison?"

Lightning's owner didn't know.

IN NINETEEN THIRTY-TWO ONE OF THOSE CASES FOR THE wisdom of King Solomon came up before a magistrate in a New York police court. Two families claimed the ownership of a black-and-tan police dog. The court ordered each group claiming the dog to different sides of the room. In the middle of the court, halfway between the rival groups, stood a patrolman with the dog on a leash.

"Now," said the magistrate, "each of you call him in turn."

"Here, Chief!" called the one man and his daughter. The dog promptly bounded over to them, apparently quite content.

Then it came the turn of the other family.

"Here, Jack," called an Italian youth and his father, both of them icemen. The dog promptly bounded back to the icemen, gleefully wagging his tail.

Next the patrolman called, "Hey, Teddie!" He was almost bowled over as the dog rushed to him.

Then the magistrate called from his bench: "Come here, Fannie!" The dog just as joyfully leaped up on the bench, and sat beside the magistrate, still wagging his tail.

Question: What to do? The magistrate was obliged to wash his hands of the whole problem. So the dog remained in the custody of the family that already had him.

In nineteen thirty-nine another of those cases for Solomon was enacted in a New York court. Two women pressed their claims for a dog. One said the pooch's name was Spot, the other said the kioodle was named Jimmy. So the wise judge, the local Solomon, stationed the two ladies on opposite sides of the court and brought the hound in. One woman called, "Here, Spot!" And the canine wandered over to her in friendly fashion. The other woman called, "Jimmy, nice Jimmy!" The mutt went over to her in an equally friendly way.

A puzzled court attendant addressed man's best friend by the name of Aloysius, and the friendly bowwow went to him in precisely the same fashion.

It certainly had the judge stopped— Solomon was stumped. But at this juncture a Negro woman called out from the crowd, "Duke! Come here, Duke!" The pup almost flew through the air. He jumped on her lap and started licking her face, his tail going as fast as an airplane propeller.

That was enough for the New York Solomon. The other two claimants made no protest as he awarded the dog to the Negro woman, saying, "His name is Duke."

Ever since the days of Uncle Tom and his Cabin, we've been taught to look upon the bloodhound as a ferocious beast. Even his name sounds fierce. However, consider the following:

In Oklahoma some officers of the law were looking for a couple of public enemies, a man and a woman who had committed several robberies. The bloodhounds were put on the traces of the two, but nothing happened. Several days later a man and a woman strolled into a restaurant. They were followed by an unusual looking but exceedingly amiable and gentle dog. The animal hunched down and watched them while they ordered breakfast.

Just as they were beginning to eat their scrambled eggs, in walked the sergeant of the Missouri highway patrol. He promptly arrested the man and woman. They were the couple so badly wanted by the law. The dog was one of the bloodhounds that had been set on their trail.

The man told the policeman: "Why, we thought that was just some farmer's coon dog. He was so friendly, we took him along."

IN FLORIDA A GANG OF FARM HANDS WAS STANDING AROUND, when Ellis Wright, big, black, and running mighty fast, came dashing right into their midst. They grabbed him, wondering what it was all about.

"Hey, boss, le' me go," panted Ellis, "I'm helping train the dogs, trainin' bloodhounds. The dogs is gettin' a lesson right now—chasin' me. And you wouldn't want to interfere with the bloodhounds' education, would you, boss?"

No, the farm hands didn't want to keep the bloodhounds from being trained, and so they let Ellis go. He disappeared over a distant hill.

A little while later the bloodhounds came along. A couple of sheriffs were with them. They were after Ellis all right, but it wasn't just training. Ellis had escaped from the county jail. They never did catch him—after he had talked his way out of a tight corner.

MR. AND MRS. WALTER USSHER OF CAMBRIDGE, MASSAchusetts, had a washing machine and a Spitz dog. They ended with a Spitz dog. This is what happened.

The dog, whose name was Pooch, was wagging her tail while Mother was doing the family washing. Pooch wagged so hard that the tail got mixed up in the machinery and tried to wag the washer. Mrs. Ussher didn't know what to do. She called in the neighbors, and they didn't know what to do. She called in the Cambridge cops, and they, always resourceful, told Mrs. Ussher she had two choices—either she could get a new dog or a new washing machine. Mrs. Ussher decided that, priorities or no priorities, she couldn't do without Pooch. So the neighbors with crowbars and sledge-hammers went to work on the washing machine. It took them three hours to set Pooch free.

THIS WAS A NEWS DISPATCH FROM KINGSTREE, SOUTH Carolina. You can take it as news—or as a tall story, just as you like. Farmer H. R. Morris had a cow that liked to switch her tail. All cows like to do that, but Farmer Morris's cow was the greatest tail-switcher in the country. And here's the sad tall story: Bossy was in the pasture, grazing beside a small tree, switching her tail as usual. She switched it so vigorously that the tail whipped around the tree and tied itself into a knot. And there was poor Bossy with her tail tied around the tree. The cow couldn't get away—and perished. That's the story, and it was told in the news as true.

REMEMBER THE OLD JOKE ABOUT THE MUSICIAN WHO AL-ways looked so sad when he played? He fiddled beautifully, but his face was like a sour pickle. Finally Maestro Toscanini said to him: "You're a fine musician, but why do you always look so gloomy when you play?"

To which the fiddler replied: "Maestro, you see—I don't like music."

[63]

That same sort of thing happened not as a joke but as the real thing. At Newark, Anthony Malizia enlisted in the army—but on one condition. "Don't put me in the cavalry," he told Recruiting Sergeant James Donovan.

"Why not?" asked the sarge.

"Well, you see," replied Tony, "I don't like horses."

"That's funny," remarked Sergeant Donovan, "what's your trade?"

To which Tony replied, "I'm a jockey."

The sergeant gasped, and Tony went on to explain. He was a jockey who had been riding thoroughbreds for prominent owners—Turfman Samuel Riddle, Motion-picture Magnate Louis B. Mayer, and Radio Crooner Bing Crosby. Tony had been riding and winning races for them —particularly at Agua Caliente, the big track in Mexico. That was pretty good going for a jockey, but Tony went on to say that recently he had acquired an acute dislike for horses. The sight of a thoroughbred or even a common nag gave him a pain in the neck. As a jockey he was like the musician who hated music. That was why he was joining the army—but not the cavalry. "No, Sergeant, please—not the cavalry."

In Newark Sergeant Donovan said okay. He signed Tony for duty in Puerto Rico with the field artillery.

THE NEW YORK AQUARIUM WAS BOTHERED BY A PLAGUE OF huge rats—ferocious rodents that preyed on the fish in the tanks. They made a specialty of eating rare specimens, precious members of the finny tribe brought from far-off waters of the tropics. So Director Christopher W. Coates decided he'd get some cats. The only trouble with the idea was that cats don't catch rats—at least not the big fighting variety that infested the Aquarium. Those critters were more likely to devour the cat. And, on the other hand, cats had an appetite for fish, as was well known. So the prospects appeared to be—that the cats would join the rats in feasting on rare fish.

Director Coates, however, was an ingenious aquarium expert. He solved the problem by getting a mountain wildcat—guaranteed to whip ten times his weight in rats. This mountain wildcat he bred with Lena, a common house cat of the mouse-chasing kind. The progeny combined the best qualities of both. They were a feline brand of rough on rats.

However, there was no guarantee that they wouldn't eat the fish. That was a problem for Director Coates to solve, and he did. He devised a course of education for Lena, the mama house cat. She simply loved fish—every day was Friday for Lena. The Director cured her of that by giving her an opportunity to enjoy what appeared to be the biggest fish Friday dish she ever had. He gave her a chance at the electric eel. Lena tried to take a bite out of the electric eel, and the shock just about blasted her out of the tank. One taste of electric eel was enough. Thereafter,

[65]

when Lena saw anything swimming in the water she'd turn tail and run. Not only that, she taught her kittens to hate fish. She just showed them the electric eel—those kittens that she had by the mountain wildcat.

As a result of all this skillful genetics, Director Coates produced a race of cats guaranteed to destroy rats and let the fish alone. The only trouble now was, that, having developed the remarkable felines, he presently didn't know what to do with them. For the old New York Aquarium was abandoned, the building torn down, the fish sent to other aquariums, and the director had to find people who would take the felines as a gift—those non-fish-eating half-mountain-wildcat pussies that had been skeered by an electric eel.

CLARENCE WARREN HAD A MONKEY, A VERY CLEVER MONKEY. Clarence had the habit of taking his intelligent pet around to stores in Chicago. And Jocko would steal articles from the counters and stuff them into Clarence's pockets. The monkey was smart and well trained—an expert shoplifter.

Clarence figured that they couldn't send a monkey to jail. Here's the way he explained it to the judge: "It isn't my fault if that fool monk kept picking things up from the counters and putting them into my pockets. Go ahead and prosecute old Jocko, if you dare. Send him to jail, if you can. Find a law for that—a law about monkeys."

The judge did send the monkey to jail. He gave him five days in the custody of the janitor of the court. His Honor sent Clarence to jail also—gave him a sentence in a common regulation hoosegow.

THE CUSTOMS GUARDS ON THE FRONTIER BETWEEN AUSTRIA and Hungary were struck by the number of young Hungarian peasant women who would cross the border every day with children in their arms. The thing that aroused their curiosity was the fact that these fond Hungarian mothers left the babies on the Austrian side when they crossed the frontier again at night to go back home. On the following morning, however, the same young women would cross over into Austria again with apparently the same baby.

So one inquisitive guard stopped a good-looking peasant damsel and investigated the baby. It wasn't a baby at all. It was a young pig. The high duties levied by the Austrian tariff on Hungarian pigs had suggested this economy to the thrifty Hungarian peasants. They would take the porkers and dress them up in babies' clothes with a handsomely embroidered bonnet covering the head. Their ingenuity went still further. In order to prevent the pigs from squealing, they first fed them with grain soaked in alcohol, which put the porkers to sleep—in a drunken stupor.

TALLY-HO! YOICKS! THE HUNTERS WERE RIDING TO THE hounds, pink coats, the traditional caps, and all the ceremonious paraphernalia of the fox hunt. Then an outrageous thing happened, most unconventional.

The Groton Hunt Club in Massachusetts was one of the most fashionable and aristocratic outfits in the country. Everything was according to form—except one fox. That mean old fellow committed the ultimate faux pas—fox pah. The hounds and the huntsmen were after him, but instead of letting himself get killed, according to the Yoicks tally-ho tradition, the fox came to bay at a stone wall. Whereupon he jumped on the back of the nearest hound and started biting and scratching. The hound howled. The other hounds turned tail and ran, with the fox chasing after them.

Then, as the huntsmen came galloping up, old Mr. Fox sat down in the middle of the bridle path and yelped defiance at the horses and riders, pink coats and all. That was the end of the Groton Fox Hunt for the day. The huntsmen followed the dogs home and the fox slid away into the woods.

You've heard of ostriches that eat hats and watches, and goats that eat tin cans. But did you ever hear of a bear that ate dynamite?

At Blacksmith Rapids, Ontario, they had a cub as a camp pet. The cub grew up, until he could pick up his masters and spank them. So they decided to get rid of him. They gave him a large dose of strychnine, but he just laughed it off. Then a doctor took a hypodermic syringe and shot enough morphine into him to send a human being farther than Rip Van Winkle ever traveled. But the bear didn't mind a bit. Finally the Greek cook at the construction camp said: "Leave him to me, boys."

The cook took the bear out into the bush, smeared honey on a stick of dynamite, gave it to the bear, and touched the fuse. Then the cook ran. There was a deafening bang, and the cook said: "Well, that's the end of your bear."

But a few minutes later, when Cookie was peeling potatoes, in walked the bear, limping on one leg, patches of hide missing, and an eyebrow gone. But the same bear.

From Grand Prairie, Texas, came the story of Lucifer the billy goat. It should teach a moral lesson. Lucifer died alone, friendless—and drunk.

He was a billy goat with a long beard and the rankest kind of smell—especially when he had liquor on his breath.

[69]

He lived with a couple of laborers named Hurley and Chapman. One night the two men set out for an evening of merriment, and they took Lucifer with them. They visited all the saloons in the town of Grand Prairie, and every time they had a drink, they gave one to Lucifer the billy goat—a shot of straight bar whisky. You've heard the expression "drunk as a billy goat." That expresses it.

Around midnight they were staggering down the street, the two men and the goat. A policeman arrested them and put them in the local calaboose, goat and all. The following morning, the two men were released on bail—but not the goat. They were all right, save for a hangover. But Lucifer was in the throes of acute alcoholism—a goatish kind of delirium tremens. Goats are known to have strong constitutions, but apparently a couple of Texans could be even more rugged.

There was no hope for Lucifer. He died a drunkard's death. Which would seem to point a temperance moral—for goats, if not for men.

A Cleveland gentleman named Reynolds shot a squirrel. He put the animal in his back pocket. Then he went hunting for more squirrels, and was hiding behind a tree to spot them. Another hunter saw the tail of the dead squirrel protruding from Mr. Reynolds' pocket, but did not see Mr. Reynolds. The other hunter fired, potted Mr. Reynolds in the southern exposure, and put him in the hospital.

AT WASHINGTON A DOCTOR WALKED INTO HIS OFFICE ONE morning, and found it in a state of chaos. Papers, records, ink, and everything were on the floor. What astonished him all the more was that against the inside of the window screen he saw two bats. He called in attendants of the building, and they started to remove the bats. The more they removed the more they seemed to find. There were bats under the window shades, bats behind the curtains, bats under the desks, bats in the corners.

When the doctor got over the shock he discovered that his centrifuge machine had been left running all night. A centrifuge machine, they say, is a thing the doctor uses for blood tests and other purposes. Well, this centrifuge apparatus, which turns round and round and round, makes a rhythmic swishing noise. The explanation was that this noise sounds something like the batting of bats' wings. The bats outside on the streets of Washington, hearing this, thought there were other bats inside the office, and came in to pay them a visit. They figured the medical sanctum was a house for bats.

A WOMAN IN CALIFORNIA HAD TO GO TO THE HOSPITAL AND was worried about what might happen to her pets while she was away. So she hired a neighbor to take care of them. After she had been in the hospital a while she went home to check up. And this is what she found:

The neighbor she had hired to take care of her pets had killed her dog, because it ate too much. He had sold her chickens. He had given away all the canaries, because they wouldn't sing. He had made the rabbits into pot pie, and sold all the goats except those that ran too fast for him to catch. With all this accomplished, he decided that the woman didn't have any use for her barn. So he tore it down and sold it for lumber. While rummaging around the basement he found an iron box containing six hundred and thirty dollars of the woman's savings. That encouraged him to go treasure-hunting, and he dug all over her land until it looked as though dive-bombers had been around.

But in one act he went too far. The woman had a horse, an aged animal of thirty years. Nevertheless, he got ten dollars for that horse. What infuriated the horse's owner most was that old Dobbin had been sold to be cut up for dog food. Now, that was a bad mistake in the West, because, as the judge informed the man when he was brought into court, the stealing of a horse, even a thirty-year-old one, was a felony in California.

The judge told the man first to give the woman her money. Whereupon he began disgorging bills from his hatband, from his shoes, from his pockets, from anything that would hold money. But all he could produce was three hundred and fifty-nine dollars—three hundred and fifty-nine out of six hundred and thirty. So the judge wanted to know where was the rest of it. The man explained that he had been under great expense. For instance, he had to feed the horse.

"But," said the judge, "you sold the horse."

"Well," said the man, "I had to feed the dog."

Said the judge: "You killed the dog."

"All right," said the man, "I had to feed the rabbits."

Said the judge: "The rabbits fed you, what do you mean?"

As the man went on to stutter out another excuse, the judge cried: "Take him to jail."

A BROOKLYN NEIGHBORHOOD HAD A PROBLEM OF BIRD LIFE and mother love. In a back yard on Wyona Street a bluejay made her nest, and in it she hatched four fledglings. When these grew big enough, they took off from the nest for their first flight. Two of them did all right, but the other two found their wings too weak and were forced down in the back yard. There one was killed by a dog. The other escaped, fluttering along the ground.

The attention of neighboring people was attracted. A man went over, picked up the bird, and tried to put it back into the nest. Mama bluejay misunderstood, and flew at him in fury, stabbing at his head and face with her beak. The would-be benefactor put the fledgling down, and made his escape. Another man tried, and he too was driven off. Two women made the attempt to put the little bird in the nest, and had to quit after their eyes were nearly pecked out.

So there in the back yard the fledgling bird remained all day, an object of the solicitude of the whole puzzled neighborhood. The dilemma ended when the bluejay attacked a ten-year-old girl who ventured too near the little bird. A man took advantage of the diversion to snare the fledgling with a net. But he didn't venture to go to the nest. He made a beeline to the humane society, and gave them the fledgling to restore to the mother bird.

Now let me get this next one straight—it's about a complicated affair of law and pigeons in Jersey City. It tells of a series of crimes and arrests about as complicated as the budget. Let's see if I can tell it without getting all tangled up.

Joseph Politowski stole fifty pigeons from Henry Grabowski. Politowski raided the Grabowski pigeon coop. Later on, Politowski sold the pigeons to a man named Samularo. Samularo gave Politowski three dollars for the fifty birds. Having got the money, Politowski proceeded to steal Samularo's automobile. As he drove away in the purloined car, Politowski picked up a friend named Savinky. Savinky took over at the wheel and was driving, with Politowski sitting beside him.

That was the state of affairs when the police stepped in. The arrests were as follows: Politowski was locked up for stealing the pigeons and the car. Samularo, whose car was stolen, was arrested for buying the pigeons—charged with receiving stolen goods. Savinky, who was driving the car, was pinched for operating an automobile while drunk.

I think I've managed to get it straight—the highly complicated pigeon case of Politowski, Grabowski, Samularo and Savinky. Correct me if I'm wrong.

*
=

THEY WERE TEARING UP THE SIDEWALK OUTSIDE ONE OF New York's old hotels. The workmen were cracking up the concrete and were beneath the first layer when one of the sledge hammers slammed on something that seemed to move. Well, it did move. It was a fourteen-pound turtle.

It had been there thirty-two years. When the sidewalk was first built outside that old New York hotel, the proprietor reported that one of his snapping turtles, which then weighed only five pounds, had disappeared. No trace of it was ever found, and it was generally supposed that the turtle had walked off somewhere. But it showed up again, not only as alive as ever, but nine pounds heavier. The mystery is—what did that turtle feed on for thirty-two years that caused it to get so fat?

*
=

ONCE MORE THE OLD STORY, "HOW HATH THE MIGHTY fallen!" The mighty one in this case being a bird, the most famous bird in England. A cockatoo—one hundred years old. Died? No, worse!

For years England knew the fame of Cocky, as he was called. He had come to England all the way from New Guinea, a gift to the grandmother of his most recent owner, Mrs. Colson. He always had his meals with the family, his own chair at the dinner table. Accompanied the family everywhere. Even round the world with them. Only once did they neglect him and leave him for twenty-four hours, alone with the servants. His pride was jilted and he wouldn't eat. He refused to take a morsel until Mrs. Colson telephoned. They put the receiver to Cocky's ear. His mistress told him by wire that he must have supper right away. Cocky jumped down and proceeded to eat the equivalent of the three meals he had missed.

Cocky achieved national fame in the World War, during a Zeppelin raid. Wounded by flying glass. His beak was broken and one eye blinded. Feathers were ripped off his breast. Thereafter his breast was naked of feathers, and he

[76]

had the scar of a wound. So Cocky was a wounded World War veteran, and enjoyed the honors. During the years that elapsed, he became more and more of a legend. Bird hero of Britain—until the humiliating event.

It turned out that Cocky's life had been a hundred years of deception. The sad secret came to light when Mrs. Colson was preparing luncheon. Cocky was perched on the table, preening and strutting. The downfall came—when Cocky suddenly laid an egg! Mrs. Colson was startled. Cocky turned around and gazed with horror at the unfortunate object. He had been glorious for all those years as a "he." Nobody ever dreamed of thinking otherwise, of questioning, of investigating—until the laying of that egg.

They had to rechristen Cocky. They called her Henrietta. And he—she, didn't like it. She strutted a hundred years as Cocky, and now—Henrietta! Every time they put that egg near Henrietta, she screeched in raucous indignation.

This dispatch from London may seem like nature faking, but things like that really do happen. I received a letter from a radio listener that went like this: "I have a yellow-headed Mexican parrot, fifteen and a half years old, and only now it has laid its first egg. We had an idea it was a male bird. Why wouldn't the parrot lay eggs before now, after all those years?"

IN CHICAGO A BEAUTIFUL BLONDE NIGHT-CLUB SINGER FILED a damage suit for five thousand dollars, and it should be a warning to bartenders—don't monkey around with frogs. The beautiful blonde told how in a Chicago bar they had a fish bowl, and in the fish bowl—a frog. A fine looking frog, the pride of the bartender. Everything was all right until a customer came into the bar, and he had his own pet frog with him. He got into an argument with the bartender. Which frog could jump the farthest—the customer's or the one in the fish bowl? They made a bet.

The bartender fished the frog out of the fish bowl, and a jumping contest was staged on the bar. After some prodding the frogs jumped. One took a mighty leap, direction somewhat wrong. The critter missed the bar, and landed in the lap of a large lady who was having a drink. When the frog bounced into her lap and presumably started jumping some more, the large lady swooned and fell off her chair. In doing so, she knocked over the beautiful blonde who was sitting next to her. The blonde fell on the floor with a crash and later charged that she became "sick, sore, lame and disordered." Everything but a frog in her throat—the fat lady almost had that, though not exactly.

ARTHUR ROSE, OF RAPID CITY, SOUTH DAKOTA, HAD A snake adventure, and I'm passing it on to you with all the sympathy in the world.

Mr. Rose climbed the bank of a stream to take a short cut home. As he reached the top he was confronted by a snake of brilliant coloring, and as slender as a lead pencil. It was a deadly coral snake. Rose reached for a rock—and grabbed a polecat, instead. But he kept his mind on the snake, and killed it. And that's what I call concentration.

*
=

THEY HAD SOME EXCITEMENT AT THE CONNECTICUT STATE Capitol. A hundred and forty-seven young women were taking tests before the State Health Department as hairdressers. Then things went bughouse.

Some lads had heard that the State Laboratory was conducting experiments with Japanese beetles. So they collected a whole lot of the pesky insects, and took them to the laboratory in the Capitol Building—hoping to sell them. They were turned down flat, the laboratory refusing to buy any beetles. That made the boys mad, and on their indignant way out they happened to notice the girls' class in hairdressing. Just why they should have wanted to take their spite out on the girls is a mystery—most ungallant. They sneaked in and turned loose their mess of beetles—and beat it.

Then it was that the hundred and forty-seven girl hairdressers suddenly discovered the swarm of bugs, crawling over the floor, crawling up their stockings. Pandemonium broke out. They screamed, crawled up on chairs, and smacked the bugs.

Peace was restored only when the janitor showed up and cleaned up the beetles with the vacuum cleaner. Then the class in hairdressing went on, with marcel and finger-waving, while the officials started a hunt—for those boys.

*
=

LONG LIVE THE QUEEN! LONG LIVE HER RATS AND MICE, cockroaches and caterpillars! The queen was Mrs. Christie, a sixty-year-old English lady. She was the monarch of Brownsea Island, a tiny speck of land off the coast of England. Her subjects were rats and mice, cockroaches and caterpillars. She loved all living things, and found it impossible to reside in England because every time she heard about somebody catching a mouse, she nearly had a nervous breakdown.

She began with a home for rabbits, millions of them—rabbits multiplying as they do. But that didn't satisfy her, so she decided to establish another sanctuary where all those creatures that the rest of mankind call vermin might have a refuge. She bought the island of Brownsea, paid half a million pounds for it, and there she ruled with her crawling, slithering subjects.

If the spiders wanted to drop from the ceiling into the soup, it was all right with the queen. The flies could swarm in the castle halls to their hearts' content, and woe unto the servant who tried to discipline them with a swatter! The queen spent all her time with her creepy subjects. She slept by day, when they slept. At night she walked by light of a candle through the castle, through the fields and woods, happy among her friends whom the rest of mankind would shrink from.

Then came the fire, and the strange kingdom lay in smoking, smoldering ruin. A three-day conflagration devastated the island. The old stone castle was saved, but the maze of other buildings went up in flame and smoke—the timber shelters where the birds nested, the nooks where bugs lived under the logs. The loss of verminous life was tremendous, and the queen's heart was broken.

＊
＝

THERE WAS AN AMAZING SPECTACLE IN CALIFORNIA. A great cloud of orange-colored butterflies, thirty miles wide, was observed crossing the state. This orange-winged army took hours to pass a given point. It was on its way from the slopes of the Sierra Nevada to better feeding grounds in the Sacramento Valley.

The butterflies were of the variety known as The Painted Lady. If you are interested in their scientific name, the entomologists identified them as Vanessa Cardui of the family known as Nymphatidae. When they flew over Tahoe, the waters of that beautiful lake reflected the color of the butterfly wings and turned to orange as far as the eye could reach.

An interesting feature of the migration was that this huge cloud of butterflies stopped traffic in Mount Lassen National Park. They gathered on the windshields and radiators of motor cars so thickly that the drivers couldn't proceed.

Rulers of Nations

THE state and majesty of sovereignty make most effective background for whims and vagaries, loves and hates, twists of sagacity and fancies of folly. Assemblages of human beings are inclined ever to hedge their Head Man with some sort of divinity, be he President or Premier, upstart despot or monarch of royal sanction—or Maharajah of India. Potentates of the Orient have an especially gaudy place in the roll-call of rulers, and the Princes of India are the most spectacular of all. But let's begin with the least gaudy.

THERE WAS A SCENE OF SIMPLICITY, SOLEMNITY AND SORrow at Hyde Park. A sunlit day, the open air, the glowing green of nature in early autumn. A church amid the trees, old trees, some of them higher than the spire of the church. A Dutchess County cemetery a hundred and thirty years old, and there the rector of St. James Episcopal Church spoke the age-old words of scriptural promise: "I am the Resurrection and the Life, saith the Lord. He that believeth in Me, though he were dead, yet shall he live. And whosoever liveth and believeth in Me, shall never die."

A small group listened with bowed heads, the President of the United States, members of his family and some friends and neighbors. Thus they bade final farewell to Mrs. Sara Delano Roosevelt, mother of the President, a woman who lived a long and ample life, with dignity and honor.

It was told by the pastor, the Reverend Frank Wilson, that the President had a strange, formless premonition the week before. With the war emergency boiling at top speed, he had intended to remain at his desk in the White House. But, as he told his pastor, he suddenly had a feeling that he ought to come up to Hyde Park, and so home he went. Thus it was that the President and the First Lady were present during the last brief illness of Mrs. Sara Delano Roosevelt.

MRS. JORDAN OF REIDSVILLE, GEORGIA, WAS RECEIVED BY President Roosevelt. From a human and dramatic point of view, that was an important bit of White House news. Mrs.

Jordan was seventy-five years old, and the doctors said she must soon lose her sight. When they told her this, she exclaimed that there was only one thing she wanted before she became blind—to see the President, while her eyesight was left. To fulfill this request they took her to Washington, and there she was disappointed twice.

She made the seven-hundred-mile trip from Georgia to the national capital, but when a Georgia Congressman inquired, he found that the presidential schedule would make it impossible for Mrs. Jordan to have an interview. The President was leaving Washington for Hyde Park. So the seventy-five-year-old woman waited at the railroad station, hoping to catch a glimpse of him as he went to the train. She missed him, however.

President Roosevelt was told the story, and he immediately placed Mrs. Jordan on his list of callers upon his return to Washington. So presently the seventy-five-year-old woman, soon to go blind, saw the President—had a visit with him.

It was an occasion for the display of the presidential gift of sympathy and understanding—that Roosevelt charm. They had a friendly heart-to-heart chat—about the South, about Georgia. President Roosevelt smilingly congratulated Mrs. Jordan on having reared a family of more than a hundred Democrats. That was true—though she never had a child of her own. She was married three times, a widow three times. Her husbands had children by previous marriages—twenty-four in all. So that gave her twenty-four stepchildren. They provided her with sixty-four stepgrandchildren. And these gave her fifteen great-step-grand-children. To cap the climax, a great-great-step-grandchild was born the night preceding her visit to the White House to see the President before she passed into darkness.

*
=

A MILITARY SECRET WAS REVEALED, A WARLIKE, HIDDEN maneuver that attended a review by President Roosevelt of the cadets at West Point. The President's aide was Colonel Edmund Watson, now a major general.

On the train the Colonel started to put on his dress uniform. As he was to accompany the President it was necessary for him to look as splendorous as Mars, the god of war. He had his epaulettes, sword, and gold braid, but where were his suspenders? The Colonel had forgotten them, left them behind. He knew that he wouldn't have any time to buy a new pair at West Point. And he certainly could not appear at the presidential dress parade without any suspenders. The possibilities are obvious, terrible to think of.

Suppose the Colonel, military aide to the President of the United States, were to lose his trousers at the dress parade. The very idea was mental torture to the Colonel. But he had a brilliant idea. He rang for the porter, the familiar, useful Pullman porter.

"George," said the Colonel, "how do you keep your pants up?"

[86]

"Why boss, ah wears suspenders."

"Give 'em to me!" commanded the Colonel. And George took off his suspenders and handed them over. I don't know about what happened to George's trousers, but the Colonel's honor was saved.

So that's how it was that the President's military aide cut a dazzling figure at the dress parade, in his own epaulettes, sword, spurs and gold braid—and the Pullman porter's suspenders.

A COUPLE OF AMHERST GRADUATES ATTENDED THE INTERnational Radio Telegraphic Conference at Madrid. One evening they decided to form the Amherst Club of Madrid, and hold their first annual dinner at the Palace Hotel. They realized that nothing would make it perfect but a message from that celebrated Amherstian, ex-President Calvin Coolidge. So they prepared a long cable to Mr. Coolidge asking him to send them a suitable message of greeting. Knowing Mr. Coolidge's frugal habits, they informed him that as delegates to the conference they had the privilege of sending free messages from Spain to the United States, also getting free replies. In short, they hinted that Mr. Coolidge need not spare any words for economy's sake.

The dinner was a great success. There were speeches humorous, and speeches sentimental. There were songs rendered with gusto. But the big moment was the reading of the message from Mr. Coolidge.

I know I mustn't make this story too long, but after all it was a message from an ex-President. So I'll print every single word of it. Here is Mr. Coolidge's message to the first annual dinner of the Amherst Club of Madrid in Spain.

"Greetings."

A REPORTER WENT TO SEE THE MOTHER OF THE MURDERED Chancellor Dolfuss, the little dictator of Austria who was killed by the Nazis. She was almost forgotten, an obscure peasant woman of an obscure Austrian village. If he was called the "little dictator," she could be called the "little mother," for she was only four and a half feet tall.

She told the reporter that she knew her boy would be murdered, and had often begged him not to become famous. He wasn't ambitious, she explained. It was a feeling of inferiority of littleness that drove him so high. When he was a boy he wanted to become a priest, but a chimney sweep told him it was no use.

"You are not tall enough," said the chimney sweep; "you are too short to wear the robes and vestments of a priest."

Yes, Dolfuss was too small to be a clergyman—so he became dictator of his country.

Here is a gibe aimed at Stalin by his bitter enemy Trotsky. It was told me by Max Schuster, publisher of Trotsky's *History of the Russian Revolution*. It seems that Trotsky decided how to dispose of his brain when he died. That sort of thing was a rather ghastly funeral custom among the Bolsheviks. Lenin started it.

As the story goes, Trotsky directed that his brain should be preserved in alcohol and sent to Moscow. There the alcohol was to be given to a friend of his, a notorious drunkard, who needed it. The brain was to be given to Stalin.

On Easter in the old city of Dublin a tall gaunt man, with deep lines in his face, made a solemn pilgrimage to a gloomy prison. In the middle of the grim prison courtyard was a plot of graves. And there the tall sad-faced man knelt for long minutes in silent prayer. This was one of the first acts in office of Eamon de Valera upon being inaugurated as President of Ireland. He paid homage to his comrades of the Easter rebellion sixteen years before—comrades condemned by a British court-martial and shot.

At the forbidding Arbor Hill Military Prison in Dublin the last tragic drama of the Easter rebellion was enacted. It was there that the leaders of the revolt were taken after they were captured. De Valera was one of them. All were sentenced to death. He was the only one to escape the firing

[89]

squad. His sentence was commuted to one of life imprisonment, because of a question of his being an American citizen. And on that day of sorrow for Ireland the volleys of the firing squad rang out repeatedly, while a nation prayed for its martyrs. The victims were buried in the cemetery at the middle of the prison courtyard.

Thereafter the Arbor Hill Military Prison was kept closed to the public, until the new De Valera regime on Easter Sunday, the sixteenth anniversary of the Easter rebellion, threw open the gloomy jail to the people. Thousands of Irish men and women visited the scene of the executions, said prayers, and laid wreaths on the graves. And among the visitors was De Valera himself, the only survivor of the men who led the revolt on Easter. He paid long and fervent homage to his fallen comrades.

IN SHANGHAI, HANCHOW, AND NANKING IT WAS A MERRY Christmas—although the slant-eyed celestials were not commemorating the Christian festival aspect of the day. There are Chinese Christians, of course, but the jubilation of the teeming millions did not concern the Star of Bethlehem. It didn't even have anything to do with Confucius. It concerned—Generalissimo Chiang Kai-shek.

For the head of the Chinese Central Government was free, turned loose by his captor, the rebellious Marshal

Chang. The Generalissimo's attractive Americanized wife had flown to the Marshal's headquarters of revolt to plead for her husband, and was with him when he returned, liberated. Strangest of all, General and Mrs. Chiang Kai-shek were accompanied by the seditious Marshal Chang. All three flew from Loyang to the government center at Nanking. The Marshal, who had staged the revolt and seized the head of the government, was giving himself up to face the music in Nanking. It's one of those weird Chinese reversals, quite incomprehensible on this side of the Pacific.

Marshal Chang, it was said, yielded unconditionally—no concessions to him. Maybe it was because the Generalissimo's wife had persuaded the Marshal not only to free her husband but also to surrender—victory of a wife's devotion. Or maybe it was the mass mobilization of Nanking troops ready for an attack. They were about to start the storm of battle: the zero hour was at hand when the Marshal yielded. So, for explanation, take your pick—a wife's devotion, or a couple of hundred thousand bayonets. Anyway, an incredible Chinese episode came to a still more incredible conclusion.

It's an old and worn-out observation that the Chinese do everything backwards. The men wear robes and the women wear trousers. They start dinner with the dessert and end with the soup. They wear white for mourning, and rejoice at funerals.

At Nanking they played the last act of the weird drama of Generalissimo Chiang Kai-shek and the rebellious Marshal Chang. The Marshal was put on trial and sentenced.

[91]

The Military Affairs Commission of the Central Chinese Government returned a verdict of—guilty. Guilty on eight charges—all eight concerned with Marshal Chang's exploit of seizing the head of the government and holding him a prisoner in an attempt to force a war with Japan. "Sentenced to be shot at sunrise," might seem to be a moderate penalty for such outrageous conduct. The sentence, however, was ten years in prison, and even that was called off, the culprit going scot free.

One point held in his favor was that he not only turned the Generalissimo loose, but himself returned voluntarily to Nanking to take his punishment. Another thing for which he could be thankful is the attitude of his victim. Chiang Kai-shek recommended mercy. You'd think the head of the government would be good and sore after being suddenly captured by a rebel general and held a prisoner while all China had a spasm of astonishment and indignation. But Chiang Kai-shek took another view of it—the Chinese view, another illustration of doing things backwards. He declared that he himself was in part to blame for the Marshal's amazing misdeed. He was at fault, he explained, because he had failed in imposing discipline upon his subordinate officer. So he made an offer to resign his offices and dignities in expiation—punishing himself for Marshal Chang's offense.

It reminds me of an episode I read about once in a Chinese history. There was an emperor who was going to the dogs, carousing all the time with wine and slave girls. He filled his palace with beauties and neglected affairs of state. What did his wife do, his empress? She considered her husband's misdemeanors, took account of all the slave girls and palace beauties—and then condemned *herself* to a dungeon. She said it was all her own fault—because she had failed to make herself charming enough to keep her husband away from the slave girls and palace beauties. Yes, a Chinese puzzle, and a Chinese wife.

It was somewhat the same in the conclusion of that fantastic affair of Chiang Kai-shek and Marshal Chang—the head of the government accusing himself of having failed to keep his subordinate in proper discipline.

*\
=

THIS IS ABOUT A KING AND CHARLIE CHAPLIN. WHAT KING? I don't know. What kingdom? I don't know that either. There was a deep secret about it all—about a few thousand feet of royal film that Charlie has in his possession.

It appears that there was a certain royal heir visiting America, and he dropped in to see Charlie Chaplin. His Royal Highness was feeling fine, and did a jovial turn in front of the camera with the plaintive little fellow with the baggy pants and big shoes. They put on a hilariously funny scene with Charlie thumping the royal anatomy and kicking the royal shins.

The prince took a copy of the film back home with him and showed it in the royal household. So presently Charlie

[93]

got a letter from His Royal Highness requesting urgently: "I beg of you never to let that film become public."

Charlie Chaplin rose to the occasion like a Machiavellian conspirator and benefactor of humanity. He wrote back: "So long as you're a good king I will keep the film secret. But if you ever become a bad king I'll give it to the Bolsheviks and let them laugh you off your throne."

Yes, the identity of that royal personage was kept a dark secret. I wonder who it could have been. What heir to a royal throne visited America? What royal prince was known for his gay and prankish ways? I've made my guess, you make yours.

THE SHAH OF PERSIA PAID A VISIT OF STATE TO THE DICTATOR of Turkey, and the focus of news was on the Shah—a tall, straight, sunbaked man with an eagle-beak nose. The story was that Shah Riza Khan Pahlevi was absolutely unique in one thing. He was the only monarch of a nation who could neither read nor write. He played his harp of statesmanship by ear.

Well, he might be as innocent as a babe of those highly decorative flourishes that constitute the Persian alphabet, he might know neither reading nor writing, but Riza Khan Pahlevi knew his onions. He was once a stable boy on the shores of the Caspian Sea. He joined up with a Russian cavalry regiment and learned about military matters from his Cossacks. His chance came when a Persian newspaper publisher decided to take over the Teheran government. The publisher hired the young Cossack to gather a band of three thousand horsemen from among the Cossack tribes on the Caspian, and staged a coup d'état.

The scheme succeeded perfectly, and young Riza Khan decided that he himself would like to be Minister of War. That was easy, but then he found out that as Minister of War his name was mud unless he could pay the Army. So he also made himself Minister of Finance. Having got that far, he thought he might as well become Prime Minister—and did so. But a Prime Minister was small potatoes beside a King, so he ousted the monarch who then occupied the Persian throne, and the ex-stable boy had himself elected Shah of Persia.

He sat on a peacock throne, and wore a gorgeous Oriental crown. He also had the most expensive car in the world, made in the U.S.A. It was upholstered in champagne-colored silk, had a gold plate body, and on each door was a golden bas-relief of the Persian crown emblazoned with green jewels.

It was too bad that the poor fellow was illiterate, as the news said he was. It must be a terrible handicap in life not to know how to read and write. A former stable boy, he sat on the throne of Cyrus, Darius and Xerxes. If that boy had only known how to spell cat, catastrophe, or cat's pajamas in Persian, he really might have got some place.

Far Eastern experts declared that Riza Khan's confabulation with Kemal Pasha was on one of the most ticklish subjects of international affairs—oil. Some of the richest oil fields lay around the border of Turkey, Persia, and the British-controlled Iraq. The British lion and also the British pipe line were in the picture, which made the picture more exciting. The well-known name Anglo-Persian Oil had an important meaning in all of this.

No wonder the two potentates lavished on each other a truly oriental hospitality. Shah Riza Khan Pahlevi made a gift to his host of three hundred bottles of the wine of Shiraz. That was Omar Khayyam's wine—of which he had a jugful and a book of poems and a gal in the wilderness, and no wonder the desert blossomed like a rose. It was about this same wine of Shiraz that Omar asked his celebrated question: "I wonder what the vintners buy half so precious as the stuff they sell." Well, that stuff more than a thousand years later was still precious. The wine of Shiraz would stand you fifteen bucks a bottle in twentieth-century Persia or Iran, as they call it now, and that is enough for a New York night club, let alone a bizarre café in Teheran, Ispahan or Shiraz.

That was a magnificent gift to Ghazi Mustapha Kemal Pasha, who, by the way, was known to like his tipple. In return Dictator Kemal, the Guzzling Ghazi, threw a party for the Persian Shah at which the diners sat on the biggest silk carpet in the world. They drank that wine of Shiraz, and then Mustapha Kemal served large quantities of the cognac of Paris, also the arrack of Iraq. Then they made speeches—

about oil, which was a different kind of liquid, but could produce a headache just as bad.

RIZA KHAN PAHLEVI FELL FROM POWER—AND PERSIAN OIL had something to do with it. He abdicated his throne, as the British and Soviet forces drew near the city that was his capital. They wanted to establish through Persia a line of supplies to the Red Army in the Nazi-Soviet War, and they wanted to secure the Iranian oil wells.

Shah Riza Khan, himself, explained his abdication with a diplomatic excuse. He said he was quitting the throne because of ill health. Everybody else knew that he was resigning because the British and Soviets were marching in and they didn't like the way he had been acting—procrastinating, dilly-dallying, trying to evade British-Soviet demands. So that's why he quit, as everybody knew. That is—everybody but the people of Iran. In Teheran there was a wise shaking of heads with sagacious smiles. They knew. They understood the real reason. It was numerology. The Persians go in for the mystical science of numbers applied to names—it's an old kind of Persian cabalistics. Years ago, they applied the mystical science of numbers to the name Riza Khan Pahlevi and found that numerology indicated

[97]

that the Shah would lose his throne in that particular year—nineteen forty-one. So that explained it all—numerology!

*
=

ALL DAY IN ETHIOPIA THE TRIBESMEN WERE GATHERING, stalwart black men, decked out in barbaric finery. In a strange old Cathedral in the capital city of Addis Ababa the successor to the throne of Solomon knelt in prayer. He and his queen prayed all night. Then, at dawn, he was anointed with oil brought especially from the Garden of Gethsemane in the Holy Land. Next Ras Tafari and his wife, Waizeru, took their places on a throne of gold, and were crowned with dazzling crowns of gold, diamonds, emeralds and sapphires. The new monarch assumed a new royal name—Hailie Selassie.

He was a small dark man. His queen was a large dark woman. Amid barbaric and imposing pomp, he became Emperor of Ethiopia, Lion of Judah, and King of Kings. He traced his descent from King Solomon and the Queen of Sheba.

While the magnificent ceremonies were going on, a sad event took place, a melancholy downfall away out in Ethiopia. The royal court was at the flying field. Hailie Selassie had an air force consisting of one plane, and this was to take a big part in the coronation ceremonies. Among those pres-

[98]

ent was an aviator, and what an aviator—Colonel Hubert Fauntleroy Julian, the Black Eagle of Harlem.

He had made Harlem headlines when he planned a flight from New York to Africa. He took off from the East River, and fell into the mud flats of Flushing Bay. Then the Black Eagle went to Ethiopia to show the new Emperor what a Harlem hero could do in the air.

He was received with suitable honors, and was at the flying field in the entourage of the newly crowned Emperor. Pomp and pageantry of African royalty—and over there stood the Abyssinian air force of one plane. The Black Eagle was seized with an inspiration. Now was the time to do something spectacular. Did he hesitate? Not he. Without asking permission, he jumped into the plane, gave her the gun, and took off.

He got up a hundred feet or so, and then the plane began to wobble. Down it came like a rocket. Crash! Bang! The crack-up occurred right in front of the Emperor, and what had been the Abyssinian air force was just kindling wood and old iron. From out of the debris crawled the Black Eagle, uninjured, grinning from ear to ear.

Was the Emperor of Ethiopia, Lion of Judah, and King of Kings, mad? He was. He ordered the Black Eagle to be clapped ignominiously into the Addis Ababa jail. Then he thought of the expense it would take to feed the hero of Harlem. He ordered the Black Eagle into instant exile. But the Black Eagle was stone broke. He didn't even have enough loose change to start a game of Ethiopian dominoes. Americans at the coronation raised enough jack to get him away, and he was led to the railroad. The Black Eagle departed with his wings clipped, claiming it was all the result of the jealousy of a French flying officer in Ras Tafari's service.

FROM THE AFRICAN JUNGLE CAME A BOOMING OF WAR drums. From the Liberian bush came a wild shout, "The King will die, but we will not surrender!" A boom-booming of war drums. From the equatorial forests came a mad wail, "The King will be hanged, but we will never surrender." And a boom-booming of war drums.

That chorus of barbaric sounds was the news in a weird tragedy of the tropical forest where wild men fight. And there was a murmur of those then familiar syllables—the League of Nations. It was the tragedy of Chief Nimley, the black lord of the Kru tribe, that somebody told him about the League of Nations—the peace and good-will society exercising its magical spell even in the "heart of darkness," as Joseph Conrad called it.

For several years there was a war to the death in Liberia, the troops of the black republic fighting to suppress the Kru tribe and its leader, Chief Nimley, terror of Liberia. He saw his villages burn, his people starve, five thousand of his fighting men killed, but he still resisted—because some mysterious white man had told him about the League of Nations. The League would bring justice for him. In nineteen thirty-two, eighty of his sub-chiefs deserted him. They surrendered to the Liberian government on a promise of safety, but they were hanged. Chief Nimley fought on, because he didn't want to be hanged, and because the white man had told him he would get help from the society for international justice at Geneva. The regiments of the government drove him and his surviving tribesmen deeper into the jungle. They starved. They ate roots and grass. But they fought on. Chief Nimley still believed in the League of Nations.

Then one day a gaunt and emaciated savage appeared out of the bush at the camp of the Liberian Army. It was Chief Nimley. They took him before the Liberian generals, and he said he wanted to surrender.

"I had seventeen sons," he related; "they were killed one by one. Now the last, the youngest, has been slain in battle. I no longer have anything to live for. I no longer believe in the League of Nations. So I am here! I have spoken! King Chief Nimley surrenders!"

They took him away to await his fate—to be hanged. He didn't care. So dispirited was he that he made a final gesture of defeat—by sending a command to the remaining handful of his warriors, saying "Surrender." The king ordering his kingless tribe finally to yield.

But in Liberia they heard the jungle answer—"No!" The war drums of the Krus gave that reply. "Our king will be hanged, but we will never surrender." That, and a boom-booming of war drums.

LONDON SOON LOST ITS MOST GLITTERING VISITOR, SIR OFORI Atta-Attaboy, in his flowing tos of plaid velvet, his thick gold crown and his tiger-skin sandals with jeweled straps. Sir Ofori Atta-Attaboy was a huge potentate with a face like a black full moon.

He was a mighty ruler from the Gold Coast of Africa. He owned diamond mines and motor cars. On the Gold Coast he walked abroad under a golden umbrella as big as a tent carried by a court officer who wore spectacles. The golden umbrella was to shield Sir Ofori's ebony complexion from the sunlight. He was knighted by King George the Fifth for leading an army of his tribesmen against Germany during the World War.

In nineteen thirty-four at great expense Sir Ofori went to London in an effort to persuade the British Government to repeal a water tax that had been slapped on his tribe. He didn't do so well in London, and he uttered a loud complaint. "The Colonial Secretary turned me down flat," he moaned. "He said 'No' to everything I asked. I stayed in London two months and he only gave me two hours of his time."

So His African Majesty left London, disappointed. And the Londoners were disappointed too. They had learned to love the millionaire African potentate, swaggering through the streets, blazing with diamonds, emeralds and gold, and spending his money freely.

TWO THINGS HAPPENED OF AN EVENING—ONE IN A NEW York hotel, the other in a fabulous oriental palace in distant Hindustan. In New York they celebrated the Diamond Jubilee of that remarkable potentate of India, the Gaekwar of Baroda. They honored him as President of the World Fellowship of Faiths, an international movement for a world religion. He had been in America some while previously, when he opened the international congress of the World Fellowship of Faiths at the Chicago Century of Progress Exposition. Then Chicago greeted him with a royal salute of twenty-one guns. Later, on the Gaekwar's Diamond Jubilee, New York honored him with a public meeting. Which was tame and commonplace beside the festivities they had in far-off Baroda. Glittering pageantry the whole week, and then, bejeweled high spot—the durbar.

Sixty years on the throne for the Gaekwar—and what a strange beginning he had! He began life as a shepherd boy, tending his flocks on remote hillsides. He was of the royal blood of Baroda, but his branch of the family had fallen on evil days. Suddenly the shepherd boy was raised to the golden throne, one of the most glittering in the world. There was a glittering story in that.

The former lord of Baroda had been a little too lavish in entertaining the British Resident at his Court, the Englishman who represented the power of the British Raj. The Gaekwar had served to the Resident a dish of food that was rather too rich. Instead of common salt, he had caused diamond dust to be used for seasoning the extravagant delicacy.

In the Orient, diamond dust is the traditional princely means of murdering an enemy. The British didn't like their pleni-potentiary to be dined in such costly fashion. So they de-throned the Gaekwar and called to the throne the other branch of the royal family, to which the shepherd boy be-longed.

Suddenly the lad found himself whisked from his hills and his sheep to the golden throne of Baroda. From a few pennies a year his personal income jumped to five million dollars a year, plus fabulous wealth in jewels—including such baubles as a carpet four yards square woven solidly of diamonds, pearls and rubies.

But the shepherd boy was, as shepherds often are, serious, thoughtful, and he wisely refrained from becoming a golden prince of feasting, rioting and squandering. Instead he went to work to make his kingdom a model state—with compul-sory education, no child marriages, the untouchables treated better than anywhere else in India. He traveled all over the world, observing, studying. As a reward, the British raised him above the royal rank of a Gaekwar of Baroda, a Prince of India. They made him a King.

His personal life was severely simple; his garb, an ordi-nary western business suit, with a Hindu cap. He arose early and ate little. He sat for hours in his library every day, read-ing English and Oriental literature and meditating. His par-ticular study was religion—the faiths of the world, a world faith.

At his durbar the princely student for once appeared in all the flaming splendor of Hindustan. Around his neck

dangled the famous two-million-dollar necklace of Baroda
that had for a pendant a huge historic diamond called the
Star of the South. All week long, during the jubilee, food
and clothes were distributed to the people. Nobody in the
kingdom was allowed to be hungry or shabby. Convicts
released, arrears in taxes wiped out. New and more progres-
sive laws were announced. Benevolent things that shone
even brighter than the two-million-dollar necklace with its
fabulous diamond, the Star of the South. Possibly it was because the Gaekwar was once a shepherd.

THE MAHARAJAH OF GONDAL WAS A DOCTOR, NOT AN ORI-
ental witch doctor dispensing powdered toads' livers or
snake-tooth amulets, but a physician out of the European
medical schools. The medical Maharajah was celebrating
his fiftieth anniversary as a ruler and doctor of his subjects
and patients.

In times gone by, the glittering potentates of India stood
shocked and aghast when they heard that the young prince,
heir to the throne of Gondal, had determined to study
the Englishman's medicine. Everybody was opposed. The
young prince disappeared. He was away for five years, taking his degrees in the medical schools of Scotland.

Then he returned. He was almost an outcast, but no one
could contest his right to the throne. So when his father

died, he became the Maharajah, and proceeded to make his kingdom sanitary. That shocked the sensibilities of the orthodox Hindus. He compelled the women of his court to unveil. He said the immemorial habit of veiling women in India was unsanitary.

He was about as popular as a cobra—until the bubonic plague came sweeping like the sickle of death. That was when the Maharajah of Medicine came into his own. He rushed the sick to hospitals, procured trained nurses to take care of them, and dispensed medicines right and left. His subjects were his patients. In plague time he was not a prince of India riding on a panoplied elephant, but a physician caring for the sick.

He checked the ravages of the bubonic horror. Victoria, Queen Empress, decorated him for his work. And what about his subjects? Well, in celebrating his fiftieth anniversary, they gave him his weight in gold. He was a thin old man, a light weight, just fifty thousand dollars' worth. He turned the gold over to a hospital.

Sir Mir Usman Ali Khan, Nizam of Hyderabad, commonly referred to as the richest man in the world, went to law and sued the owners and crew of the famous Italian salvage ship, the *Artiglio*. The tale began with the sinking of a British liner off Cape Ushant. The ship went to the bottom of the choppy waters of the English Channel, carrying with it a consignment of gold and banknotes belonging to His Highness, the Nizam. Shortly after the sinking, the lost banknotes were canceled, and the Nizam's treasury printers turned out a new issue.

Then the salvagers of the *Artiglio* got on the job. They raised not only the gold but also the iron chests tightly packed with three and a half million dollars' worth of the Nizam's paper money. The Nizam didn't want the banknotes back, since they had been canceled. So members of the crew improved the shining hour by selling them all over Italy as souvenirs. That's what annoyed the Nizam. He refused to pay for having the banknotes salvaged, he sued the owners and crew of the *Artiglio*. He said he gave no instructions for the canceled currency to be brought up from the briny deep. It cost him money to have the new issue printed, and he certainly didn't tell the sailors to go around hawking the obsolete paper money.

The richest man in the world was said to be in many respects a tightwad. Once every year a van laden high with gold bars was driven into an underground cellar beneath the palace. It was parked next to a similar van also full of gold, and there it stayed. A gold coin that passed into the royal clutches just passed out of circulation. Nothing but paper money and small coin was used in the huge state ruled by His Highness.

He never wasted a penny. Nothing in his palace could be thrown away until the royal eyes had inspected it and decided that it could no longer be used. He drove about in ancient flivvers that rattled like skeletons bouncing on a tin roof. He wore the shabbiest clothes in his kingdom, leaving glorious raiment and Sultanic splendor to his servants—except on state occasions, when he turned himself into a picture out of an oriental story book.

ABOARD A VESSEL INDIA-BOUND FROM LONDON WERE FORTY-eight of the largest and flattest feet in Europe. Twenty-four Scotland Yard detectives on their way to Hyderabad, fabulous principality of the Deccan in Hindustan. Deep mystery surrounded their departure. Nobody knew why that consignment of two dozen sleuths should have been shipped to the King-Emperor's Indian Empire. Then the mystery was dispelled. They were going out to protect the heir of the richest man in the world, His Highness, the Nizam.

It seemed that His Highness had been reading American newspapers and looking at gangster pictures, and the idea struck his august mind that some knowledge of the technique of American snatchers may have trickled into the heads of other people in India beside himself. In short, His Highness had become afraid of kidnapers. Not so much on his own account, but on account of his tiny grandson, an infant whose value was estimated at five hundred million dollars. So it was to serve as bodyguards for that gilded baby that the forty-eight sleuthing flat feet were sailing.

I happened to see a picture of that infant Croesus. The little chap looked more like something out of the *Arabian Nights* than a live baby. Carried in the arms of his ayah, he was dressed in cloth of gold so rich and jewel-encrusted that it would have made a grown man stagger if he had tried to wear it.

Nobody knew how rich the Nizam really was—nobody, including himself. The legend persisted that the bulk of his wealth, jewels collected by his ancestors of hundreds of years, was kept in a mysterious cave, a cave like the famous one invaded by Ali Baba. It was supposed to be guarded by poisonous snakes—cobras and Russell's vipers. Only the official custodians knew the password that the snakes understood.

Whenever a wedding took place in the Nizam's family, his sons and daughters were allowed to go into the cave and take away as many jewels as they could carry in their hands. But when they died, the jewels were returned to the cave. One of the latest of such marriages was that of the Nizam's eldest son. He was the father of the baby with the bodyguard of twenty-four European flat feet. His name was Sahabizada Azam Jab. The lady he married, the five-hundred-million-dollar baby's mother, was the Princess Darru Shavar, only daughter of the late Prince Abdul Medjid Effendi, former Caliph of the Moslems and legal successor of the Sultans of Turkey.

THEY HAD A BIG TIME IN ENGLAND. THE THREE THINGS that solid Britain took most seriously were the King, the Empire and horse racing, and the jockeys rode the galloping ponies in the Saint Leger Stakes, one of England's major racing classics. The winner was Windsor Lad. As Windsor Lad had also won the Derby his victory in the Saint Leger Stakes made him England's greatest horse. It also made an Indian Maharajah England's greatest horseman. The Maharajah of Rajpipla, the wealthy prince of India who owned Windsor Lad, was the toast that night of England's horsey millions.

The Maharajah of Rajpipla was the ruler of a kingdom not far from Bombay, with powers of life and death over a quarter of a million people. He spoke perfect English and played polo. When he was in England, he lived next door to the King's own Windsor Castle.

They told a story of how the Maharajah of Rajpipla at the Derby one year met a sprightly New Yorker named Jerry Maguire. They became a couple of pals, and Jerry Maguire said to Rajpipla, "Raj, when you're in New York, come up and see me sometime."

In due time, the Monarch of Rajpipla did visit New York and started to look up Jerry Maguire. There were scores of Maguires in the New York telephone book. Everybody he met knew somebody named Maguire. There were just too many Maguires. So, after three months' search, it was said, the Maharajah of Rajpipla gave an exhausted "pip-pip" and went home to Rajpipla.

I told that on the radio, and got a prompt correction from

Jerry Maguire. Over the telephone Jerry admitted that there are plenty of Maguires, all right, but added that the Maharajah found *the* Maguire.

"It was back in 1928," Jerry related. "I took the Maharajah to Washington and Chicago and showed him the sights. He sure liked America," said *the* Maguire. "He bought every make of automobile and typewriter he could find."

Now about the trunks and trumpets—meaning elephants. They have trunks and sure can trumpet. Such was the theme of a sad, sad story, of how an oriental sultan lost his job. A mighty potentate was the Sultan Shamshudeen Iskander, Lord of the Maldive Islands, Prince of Coral Seas, and Emperor of Coconut Groves. He reigned in glory over his remote little archipelago way off in the Indian Ocean, midway between Africa and India.

Then the news came—he had lost his throne. I for one was sorry to learn of it, because I first heard of the Sultan of the Maldives in a thrilling and sympathetic tale of adventure. It was told me by Captain Guy Smith, an American aviator with whom I was flying when he was a military pilot with the British during World War days along the Red Sea.

With an observer he flew out over the Indian Ocean one day, and was forced down on a strange island, nowhere near anywhere. After a terrifying time of it, they were taken by natives to another island, where the oceanic Sultan of the Maldives kept his barbaric court. To their amazement, the two castaways were honored with kingly hospitality, were given the freedom of the Sultan's palace, and finally, to cap the climax, were decked in oriental finery and made members of the local Maldivian House of Lords. The reason, though they didn't know it, was that the Sultan of the Maldives had made a treaty with Great Britain, in which he bound himself to be kind to shipwrecked mariners or stranded aviators who might be cast on his shores. The Sultan was doing it up brown. It was his first chance.

His Majesty, Shamshudeen Iskander of the Maldives, was a royal personage to behold, a giant of six feet seven, with as splendid a spreading beard as ever covered a true Moslem's bosom. He could out-wrestle any man in his kingdom, and with a pistol seldom missed the bull's-eye. And his garb was always of the best. That was part of the trouble.

Sometimes he wore a fabulously glittering native costume. Perhaps his subjects didn't mind that so much, but in his contact with the British he had acquired western ideas, and cultivated a taste for London tailoring. He had a hundred and forty-seven suits of clothes from the most expensive West End tailors. He needed them, because he changed his costume every two hours throughout the day.

Briefly the Sultan had expensive habits and these expensive habits came to a climax when he went in for a stable. Not a stable of horses—a stable of elephants. He was a magnificent judge of elephant flesh, and collected the best and most costly pachyderms from all over the East. Also scores of crack mahouts from Bengal and Burma. His elephants' turnouts blazed with jewels and gold. He poured the royal treasury into the royal elephant stables—a million rupees at a time, they say.

It all caused the local Maldivian taxes to soar, while the Maldivian taxpayers groaned and squawked. At last they could bear it no longer. The Sultan's loyal subjects ceased to be loyal. So they deposed him—a throne lost because of the siren lure of the waving trunks and the loud trumpeting of elephants.

THERE ARE ALL SORTS OF UNIONS IN THE WORLD, AND IT might seem difficult to invent a new kind of unionization. Here it is, though—a proposal to form a union of ex-sovereigns, kings and queens in exile. That would be interesting, dethroned royalty exercising the right of collective bargaining; and, picketing? Kings and queens in the picket lines, carrying sandwich signs saying, "This place is unfair to organized royalty!"

The proposal was made in Paris by former Queen Salimba Machimba. In case you haven't heard of Her ex-Majesty Salimba Machimba, she once was monarch of the Island of Moheli. And in case you never heard of the Island of Moheli, it's a speck of land with some coconut groves way down in the Indian Ocean, off Madagascar. Queen Salimba Machimba complained that kings and queens in exile were not being treated fairly—unfair practices, as our Wagner Labor Act puts it. They were not getting enough royal salutes and regal entertainment, but, as usual, it was really a case of wages.

Years before, Queen Salimba Machimba had transferred her coconut sovereignty of the Island of Moheli to France. In return she was guaranteed a royal pension—many French coconuts. She still got it, but inflated currency had cut its value so much that the pension was not royal any more. It was quite plebeian—the French coconuts had shrunk. So Salimba Machimba issued a call for exiled royalty to unionize—and protect their pensions and perquisites, if any. Union Organizer Salimba Machimba was backed by the former Sultan of Turkestan and the ex-Amir of Afghanistan. They all wanted union cards. So announced Her ex-Coconut Majesty, Queen Salimba Machimba.

THEY OPENED THE TOMB OF TUT-ANKH-AMEN, AND A young English newspaperman was out to get the story. He was Valentine Williams, war correspondent and author of mystery novels. He relates the following:

"It was my biggest scoop, my luckiest break. You remember King Tut's tomb? In the crypt they found a sealed door. The whole world was waiting breathlessly to know whether the chamber beyond that door was empty or whether the

King's mummy lay behind it. That was what I was sent to Luxor to find out. It was an almost desperate mission. You see, the London *Times* had bought up the story from Lord Carnarvon, and other newspapers had to take the news from the *Times* or go without. I represented a rival paper. Carnarvon told me quite frankly I was wasting my time—nobody except the *Times* would be told anything. The tomb was barred to everybody except the excavators, and I felt pretty blue.

"Carnarvon said nothing about his plans, but I managed to discover that the sealed door was to be opened on a certain Friday. So I went ahead just as though I was sure of getting the story. To reach the tomb you had to cross the Nile in a boat and ride seven miles on a donkey, through the hills. Well, the fateful Friday came, and I was there—waiting outside the excavation. After lunch, Carnarvon, at the head of the digging party and a group of invited guests, descended into the tomb. With despair in my heart I listened to muffled knocking in the bowels of the earth. I had no story and saw no prospect of getting it.

"Then fortune smiled. A fat Egyptian pasha came waddling out of the tomb for a breath of air. It was my only chance, and I seized it. Trying on him one of the oldest tricks of the trade, 'Excellency,' I said, 'did they find more than one coffin?' 'No, only one,' he replied without guile. 'Very beautifully decorated, isn't it?' I persisted. 'Marvelous,' he wheezed. 'All blue and gold!'

"Then he realized that I was pumping him and fled. But I had my story, and within five seconds my flash with the news that King Tut's sarcophagus had been found was on its way. It was the first message to leave Luxor, and in New York and London the evening papers were on the streets with the news before the excavators left the tomb. Poor Carnarvon died a few weeks later without ever knowing how I did it."

To this narration the record adds that the untimely death of Lord Carnarvon began a series of luckless mishaps that created a legend of the curse of Tut-Ankh-Amen.

EGYPTIAN PHARAOHS HAVE A WAY OF PUTTING CURSES ON tombs, it seems. A weird yarn came from Edinburgh, told by a British soldier and diplomat, Sir Alexander Seton. While in Egypt, Lady Seton was present at the opening of the tomb of one of the ancient Pharaohs at Gizeh. As a souvenir she brought back a fragment of bone. Soon after her return to her home in Edinburgh, Lady Seton visited a soothsayer who warned her that misfortune was hanging over her house. She told her husband, who scoffed at the idea.

Two months after that, people living in the house became afflicted with a sudden and unexplainable illness. Fire broke out twice in baffling circumstances. Presently, stories circulated around Edinburgh that the house of Sir Alexander Seton was unlucky. Maids refused to work there. House guests reported that strange noises had aroused them in the middle of the night. One of them even saw a ghost. Glassware crashed at spooky hours for no good reason.

Sir Alexander Seton still said that superstition was nonsense. Nevertheless, he gave that relic from the tomb of the Pharaohs to a friend, a surgeon. Two days later the surgeon returned the gift. And in explanation he said that his cook had seen a tall white-swathed figure, for all the world like a mummy-come-to-life. The apparition chased his cook, she ran and broke her leg.

So Alexander Seton took the bone, and put it back in the glass case he had had made to contain it. The following day he was telling a friend about it. The friend said: "I should like to see it."

"Come upstairs," said Sir Alexander.

Thereupon, in Sir Alexander's own words: "As we approached the door we heard a muffled noise. Upon opening the door we found the glass case lying near the door on the table. The glass was pulverized as though it had been ground under somebody's heel. The bone lay halfway out of the case."

It was all the more puzzling because the table was only two feet high, the floor was thickly carpeted, and nobody had been in the room.

IN THE QUAINT OLD WALLED CITY OF AVIGNON, IN THE south of France, lived an old-time actress, famous in her day, on whom the French Government pinned the Legion of Honor. Madame Vorns-Baretta had strutted the stage for many a year, a favorite at the famous Comédie Française. When she was rewarded with the glamorous decoration created by the great Napoleon, people said it was doubly appropriate, because in the family of the actress they still had an unpaid bill incurred by Napoleon.

The amount of the bill was sixty francs. It was for food and wine which Napoleon bought and never paid for, and sixty francs bought a lot of omelet, ragout, and vin rouge ordinaire or extra-ordinaire in those old days nearly a century and a half ago.

Hippolyte Baretta, the grandfather of the actress, was the keeper of a tavern in the city of Popes, the high-walled city of Avignon. Napoleon was then a young and obscure artillery officer. He was on his way to the Siege of Toulon, where he performed so brilliantly against the British that he laid the foundation of that magical reputation that was later to make him Emperor of France, master of Europe, and hero of the age. He passed through Avignon and stopped at the tavern of Hippolyte Baretta for dinner. Napoleon was a skinny, hungry youth in those days, but just the same he wasn't likely to eat and drink sixty francs' worth at one meal. He was full of big ideas, however, and he didn't mind telling the world just what was what.

In the tavern of Avignon he explained his political ideas

to the boys who were hanging around. There was a grand argument. Then the young Napoleon invited several sympathetic listeners to have dinner with him. He treated them to the best in the place. They ate and drank heartily. And all the time he told them what was wrong with France and what was wrong with the world, and how he would run things. It was a noble and inspiring occasion, but when it was all over, along came the inevitable, that sad event to which all good times lead—the bill, the check, the sad news.

Hippolyte added up the figures and presented the fiery young Bonaparte with a bill for sixty francs. The man who was to become the master of the world fished into his wallet. It was the same old story, the sad old story—he didn't have the money.

Ah, yes, it was too bad. Monsieur the innkeeper would understand. The paymaster of the Republic was a scoundrel, he was always late. Lieutenant Bonaparte had pay coming to him, but he hadn't been able to collect it yet. Would the good innkeeper be kind enough to wait until the paymaster had done his duty, and Lieutenant Bonaparte would send him the sixty francs.

Yes, Hippolyte Baretta, the innkeeper, said he would wait. I guess that was about all he could say. And Bonaparte went on to the Siege of Toulon. He didn't know it, but he was on his way to an imperial crown.

He forgot all about those sixty francs. In the hurly-burly of battle and the affairs of state, Napoleon forgot that small debt. The innkeeper thought it would be perhaps not in the best of taste to present a bill to the man who was conquering Europe. He kept the slip of paper, with the figures on it, as a memento.

So it was only a bit of poetic justice that those many years later his granddaughter should be granted the decoration that Napoleon had created, the Legion of Honor.

HERE'S ABOUT AN EMPEROR, HIS MAJESTY, NORTON THE First, Emperor of the United States and Protector of Mexico. No, I'm not dizzy. The emperor *was!*

Out in California they planned a monument to His Majesty, Norton the First. With all solemnity they gave him a second funeral, from the Masonic Cemetery, where he had been buried for many a long year, to the Woodlawn Memorial Park.

He was unique among the world's monarchs, an English Jew who came to California from South Africa during the gold rush of '49. At first, Joshua Norton had no imperial dreams, not even gold-camp dreams of gold. He built his ambition on rice. For in California of the gold camps John Chinaman, the celestial cook and Far Eastern washy-washy man, was a familiar, friendly figure. The old Wild West was full of the "heathen Chinee." And the "heathen Chinee" needed rice. So Joshua Norton schemed a monopoly of rice. He had the rice market cornered, when two big boatloads of rice arrived unexpectedly at San Francisco from the Orient. That busted the corner on rice. It also busted Joshua Norton—busted him financially and busted him a bit mentally. He was never quite the same in the head afterwards.

He disappeared. No more was seen of him in the California gold camps for years. When he returned, he was a different man—he was an emperor. He wore a shabby naval uniform of faded blue. A tarnished saber in a rusty scabbard dangled at his side. He was always accompanied by two huge ferocious dogs, guardians of his throne. He announced that the California legislature had made him Emperor of California. But he didn't want to frighten the government at Washington. He didn't want them to think he was having California secede from the United States. He was too smart for that. He declared himself Emperor of the whole United States. He also liked the Mexicans. So he declared a protectorate over Mexico.

Those were the expansive days of the old Wild West, full of generosity, lawlessness, shooting, and good humor. The gold miners were amused by Emperor Norton the First. They liked him, honored him, entertained him, paid mock homage to him. He and his two huge dogs dined free at the restaurants. Banks even cashed his checks, which he shrewdly kept quite small. Maybe he wasn't so cuckoo after all. He made visits to the California legislature and was allowed to sit among the lawmakers in the front row. There he solemnly proclaimed his royal edicts, which were duly printed in the newspapers among other legislative transactions. One of his edicts, prophetically enough, commanded the building of a bridge which sixty-three years later was actually built and dedicated by President Hoover.

For the rest of his days His Majesty Norton the First, Emperor of the United States and Protector of Mexico, was treated with good-humored honor. Public sentiment wouldn't tolerate any disrespect toward him. When he died, his loyal subjects raised ten thousand dollars and gave him an imperial funeral.

He still lives on in California, a dim droll legend of a dim bygone time. Long live the memory of Norton the First, Emperor of the United States and Protector of Mexico!

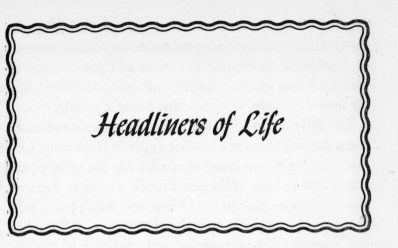

Headliners of Life

THIS is a celebrity-worshiping era, and tales told of those that are blazoned by fame are esteemed the most highly. Politician, literary light, millionaire, explorer, titled aristocrat and sports idol—I don't know whether their woes evoke a larger tear, but their absurdities do get a bigger laugh. Woes and absurdities are tacked to famous names in full measure—with all gradations of mood in between.

ONE OF THE ASTONISHING THINGS ABOUT MAHATMA Gandhi is the quality of some of the converts he has made. For example, English and American women of wealth and high position who have become devotees of the ascetic

Hindu philosophy propounded by the little brown man in the loin cloth and have adopted the extraordinary practices of East India mysticism. The prize and pre-eminent example of this was the English admiral's daughter about whom reams were written—Miss Madeline Slade.

The story began when she was a society beauty of aristocratic Britain. She was a familiar figure in fashionable London drawing rooms, handsome, with big brown eyes, and was considered one of the best-dressed women in England. She went on a cruise to the Orient, and didn't come back. She joined Gandhi. She took the Hindu name of "Mirabai" and became a close co-worker and confidant of the Mahatma.

When she returned to England, she astonished her former fashionable friends by traversing the streets barefoot, with the characteristic Indian garb of cotton sheeting for a gown.

Her continued and ever-increasing devotion to Gandhi's gospel brought her to the United States. She went on a coast-to-coast lecture tour which she described by saying: "I will speak about my master, Gandhi, and my beloved adopted country, India."

In the U.S.A. she continued strictly her ascetic Indian way of life—rising at four o'clock each morning for prayers to the gods of Hindustan, and eating only bread and butter and a few boiled vegetables. She did not even allow herself a cup of tea, although she admitted that the good old London afternoon spot of tea was the hardest habit to break.

There was a wealthy American woman, Miss Nila Cram Cook, who became a devotee of the Mahatma, but it didn't last. She came back to the U.S.A., declaring that she was disgusted. She was tired of being Gandhi's Blue Serpent Goddess, which she said was her title in Hindu mystic circles.

She got into a controversy with the British Admiral's daughter. That happened when Miss Madeline Slade, known by the melodious Hindustani name of Mirabai, arrived in the United States to preach the doctrine of Gandhi. In fact, the Blue Serpent Goddess and Mirabai had a regular hair-pulling match—only there wasn't much hair to pull. It narrowed down to a matter of shaved heads, both ladies having had their crania shaved as smooth as Jim Farley's. That was a part of Gandhi's spiritual doctrine.

First, Mirabai gave her opinion of the Blue Serpent Goddess: "I think she tried to turn herself into a saint, and it must have been a strain on her mind."

To which the Blue Serpent Goddess responded: "Mirabai doesn't like me, because I didn't choose to go through all my life with a head like a hard-boiled egg. We both shaved our heads, but after the required time elapsed I let my hair grow back. She calls that a moral fall."

It was a heady argument.

The rumpus among Gandhi's disciples was nothing beside the trouble caused by his son. The seer and saint of India practiced an Oriental philosophy of patience, of passive longsuffering. He had gone through many an ordeal, prison, humiliation, disappointment, but I don't suppose anyone gave him a heavier burden to bear than his son Hiralal. For Hiralal, son of Gandhi, turned against his fa-

[125]

ther and against the religion of Hinduism, of which Gandhi was a fervent apostle. Hiralal became a Moslem. He joined the Mohammedans, those arch enemies of the Hindu religion. Hiralal, in his Islamic fervor, made a speaking tour, publicly denouncing the doctrines of his father.

Still worse, Hiralal took to drink. That was odd, because Islam was strictly a prohibitionist religion; all alcoholic beverages were forbidden by the Koran. However, the word from India was that Hiralal, after his conversion to Mohammedanism, went on a long series of Hindustani benders. Quite a wayward young Moslem or Hindu—or what? You can fancy the scandal all this made in India and what a heartbreaker it was for Mahatma Gandhi.

Then there was a change for the better—thanks to Gandhi's wife, Hiralal's mother. She made a solemn public appeal to her wayward son. And it worked. Hiralal went back in sorrow and repentance, making peace with his father, making peace with Hinduism. So Gandhi and his son Hiralal were on proper paternal and filial terms once more. There was a solemn ceremony in which Hiralal, renouncing Islam, was taken back into the fold of Hinduism. Hiralal was purified.

THE MOTORCYCLE ACCIDENT THAT ENDED THE LIFE OF LAWrence of Arabia was but a tragic culmination of the main theme that had dominated his career—Lawrence's desire for obscurity, his singular hatred for publicity and the limelight of acclaim. That phase of his character impressed me vividly when I knew him during World War days, the time of his almost fantastic leadership of raiding and campaigning in the desert. He would come to British headquarters as spokesman for his Arab army, but he shied away from public notice.

I recall how, right after the war, when I was telling the story of "Lawrence of Arabia" from the public platform in London, he came one night, shyly, avoiding attention, almost sneaking in. So it was not surprising to hear in the years that followed how Lawrence in singular ways was trying to bury himself in anonymous oblivion, hiding away as a private in the Royal Air Force under the name of Aircraftsman Shaw—the beam of limelight always seeking him out while he fought to avoid the public glare.

All of this was the subject of discussion when I encountered Colonel Ralph Isham, long-time friend of Lawrence. When one met Colonel Isham one expected to hear something interesting about books and about the makers of books. He was a noted bibliophile who made literary history by discovering a famous store of Boswell manuscripts, unknown writings left by that racy biographer of Dr. Johnson. They were tucked away in a strange old Irish castle. Books had been the interest which had drawn together the Oxford scholar and the American bookman.

As we sat talking, Ralph Isham described a visit that he

had paid to Lawrence, in England shortly after Lawrence's term in the Air Corps had expired. The man of legend had gone to his secluded cottage in Dorset. So to Dorset the Colonel went. He told me how he had driven to the Lawrence cottage and of the singular impression made on him, as the car rounded the wooded curve in the road. He saw a number of city clad men grouped about—as if in serious deliberation.

"I had never seen a more charming place than Lawrence had picked for his retirement," he said. " At the foot of a steep hillside, almost buried in rhododendron bushes, a fine old stone cottage, with a marvelous tiled roof. I knocked, no answer. Then I shouted for Lawrence. No result. Next I noticed some broken tiles on the ground near the cottage. They were from the roof, shattered bits of tile—so old and fine, they were almost like jewels. I wondered what the deuce it was all about. At last, a man, a farmer, came along. He said he was taking care of the place of Colonel Lawrence, and he told me what had occurred.

"Lawrence had been followed to his Dorset retreat by news photographers. They had besieged his place. He had resented the intrusion. They had come banging on his door, demanding that he pose for them. He had punched one fellow and given him a black eye. Then the photographers had set a trap. They had hid a camera in the rhododendron bushes, had set it in to cover the cottage door, so that they could snap a picture of Lawrence when he emerged. And they had gone about finding a way to get him to come out. A couple of them had climbed up the side of the hill above the cottage, and tossed rocks down on the roof. They had flung a barrage of rocks, smashing the tiles. That was the meaning of the fragments of tile I saw on the ground.

"The caretaker told me that Lawrence, by means of strategy, had been able to get away from the place, unphotographed. He had said—'I'll be back when you see me.' The photographers were still besieging the cottage, not knowing that he had escaped. That was the reason for the men I saw lurking near the house.

"Five days later Lawrence came to see me in London, and spent the afternoon with me. He told me that he couldn't go back to his Dorset place, for the present, because they wouldn't leave him alone there. So he was going off by himself on his push-bike. He said he intended to make a tour around England until the fuss had died down. Then he would return to his cottage. That was the last I ever saw of him. He did go back to his Dorset place, eventually, and there, while he was riding on his motorcycle between the cottage and the neighboring village, the accident occurred.

"As I look back on it now," Ralph Isham concluded, "it was all a part of his yearning to escape—his never-ending, never-accomplished flight from publicity. He met his fate in an attempt to escape his fame."

Many Englishmen thought that Lawrence of Arabia should have been buried in Westminster Abbey, but he was buried in a Dorset countryside grave without even a nameplate on his coffin. His friends knew this would have been his wish. There were no brilliant uniforms worn, no guards of honor. But there were pageant and romance in the mere names of those who were there.

One of the mourners was a representative of the King of Iraq. Without Lawrence, young Ghazi would not have been ruling in Baghdad. For he was the son of Feisal, the Arab Emir who owed two thrones, Syrian and Mesopotamian, to the pink-cheeked, blue-eyed Lawrence. At the grave was a representative of Emir Abdullah, the Sultan of Transjordania. He too ruled because of the success of the desert revolt led by Lawrence.

Another at the grave was my old friend Jaafar Pasha, Iraq's minister to Britain, the same jolly old Jaafar who was a general in the Turkish Army, was captured by the British, broke his leg trying to escape from the prison citadel in Cairo, and afterwards volunteered to serve with the Arabs against the Turks. I knew him when he was the commander of all the regular, drilled forces under Lawrence.

Winston Churchill was there, the man who forcibly had pulled Lawrence out of retirement after the World War. Churchill placed him in charge of Near Eastern affairs at the Colonial Office. Lawrence reluctantly agreed to help Churchill for a year. When the year was up, no one remembered the time had expired—that is, no one but Lawrence. He, without saying a word to anyone, put on his hat and walked out—into retirement again, the retirement that took him first into the Tank Corps and then into the Air Force as a private soldier under an assumed name, to escape the limelight.

The Earl of Winterton was there, the gallant British lord who grew himself a fierce black beard and helped Lawrence in the desert campaign. Later he became one of the leading peers in the King's realm.

There also stood Augustus John, one of the great artists of our time, who delighted to paint Lawrence in his Arab robes. And Lord Lloyd, British proconsul and ruler of empire, sometime Governor of Bombay Presidency in India, and High Commissioner of Egypt. In World War days we in Arabia knew him as plain Captain George Lloyd, just another young officer associated with Lawrence and the Arabs.

Two women saw Lawrence to his last rest. Mrs. Thomas Hardy, widow of the world-renowned novelist. Her husband had been one of Lawrence's few close friends. And Lady Astor, who on her last previous visit to America had told me how she had ridden double with Lawrence on his motor-bike, the same one on which he rode to his death.

There were six pallbearers at the funeral—and what a story could be written around them! Patrick Knowles, the batman, the boots, who had looked after T. E. during the last few years. Eric Pennington, the young artist whom Lawrence, at great expense, had sent to the Near East to paint portraits on the spot of old Sheik Auda Abu Tayi, the Arab robber, and others with whom the young Englishman had fought—the pictures he used in his *Seven Pillars of Wisdom* and *Revolt in the Desert*.

There were two pallbearers whose names brought stirring memories back to me. I had known them well. Sir

Ronald Storrs, who in Jerusalem first introduced me to Lawrence. And Colonel S. F. Newcombe, Lawrence's fighting predecessor. He helped the Arabs against the Turks before the young Oxford don arrived on the scene. He was one of the most spectacular figures of the war in the East. The Turks captured him. Later, with the aid of a beautiful Levantine girl, he escaped from prison in Constantinople —and the gallant dashing Colonel married the girl.

Such were the pallbearers who carried the coffin without the nameplate; the coffin on which were placed no flowers except one bouquet of lilacs and forget-me-nots. These were from a young girl, who sent them with the inscription: "To T. E. L., who should sleep amongst the Kings."

A TRAGIC SHADOW WAS SUMMONED, THE GHOSTLY FIGURE of Edith Cavell, and in the foreground were two living people—a man released from prison and a quiet, secluded French schoolmistress.

The man was Gaston Quien, who was said to have betrayed Nurse Cavell to the Germans. He was accused of having given them the information that she was harboring escaped war prisoners. After the war the man was tried for this, and sent to prison—protesting his innocence. Twenty years later he was released. Why? Because the authorities at that late date found that the evidence against him in that trial of long ago had been insufficient. There was doubt that it had actually been Gaston Quien who had betrayed Nurse Cavell.

There was one person who perhaps might be expected to know—the French schoolmistress. She presided over an academy for girls on the outskirts of Paris. Her name was Louise Thuliez, a name linked on the tragic record with that of Edith Cavell. She had worked with the English nurse in Belgium. Miss Cavell and Mademoiselle Thuliez had been partners in helping escaped war prisoners, and they both had been tried by the German court-martial, and sentenced to death.

Edith Cavell was immediately executed in that episode of terror that stirred the wrath of the world. In the outcry that followed, the life of Mademoiselle Thuliez was spared —because of urgent representations made by President Wilson, the Spanish ambassador to Brussels, and the Pope. Her sentence was commuted to imprisonment. She spent thirty-three months in a cell, and was released three days before the Armistice. The Allied governments decorated her with an array of medals, among them the Croix de Guerre and the Order of the British Empire. Later she became the head mistress of a school of fifty girls. She seldom spoke, keeping her silence about those events of other days.

When Gaston Quien, the man accused of betraying both Edith Cavell and Louise Thuliez, was released, Mademoiselle Thuliez was asked: What did she think? She denounced the execution of Nurse Cavell, and said it was merely an act of German bitterness against England. The deed was

[133]

carried out even before the official notice of the sentence was published. The sentence was unjustifiable, the haste unforgivable—so said Louise Thuliez.

But what about the man, Gaston Quien? The quiet little schoolmistress shook her head—she could not judge. Was he guilty? Was he the man who betrayed her and Edith Cavell to the Germans? Or did he stand a tragic figure of innocence, after twenty years in prison, after having been branded with the infamous crime of treason? Louise Thuliez could not answer those questions. She did not know. So all that remained was—doubt.

THE BRITISH AUTHORITIES HAD A SURPRISE WHEN THE CAnadian Pacific liner, *The Duchess of York*, docked at Liverpool. They were looking for one thing, but they found something else. It was in the days of Dillinger, and America's Public Enemy Number One was rumored to be aboard the ship. A strong detachment of Scotland Yard sleuths made a thorough search. But they didn't find Dillinger. Instead, they found a Buddhist ecclesiastic, the Abbot Jochao Chao-Kung. But the British immediately recognized the oriental holy man as their old friend Ignatius Trebitsch Lincoln, one of the fantastic figures of the World War, former British member of Parliament and—also a German spy.

He was most interesting, however, not in connection with espionage—but with religion. He was born a Jew, became a Lutheran, then a Presbyterian, and later joined the Church of England, in which he became a curate. Then he turned Quaker. Next he tried religion in the Orient. He also did some gun-running and became financial adviser to a Chinese general. More recently he had been prominent as a member of the imperial court of Manchukuo. Finally—a Buddhist monk.

This was the interesting gentleman whom the British found in place of Dillinger. He had with him six Buddhist monks and four nuns. His intention, he said, was to found a Buddhist colony in England. To the British he was just an undesirable adventurer—a renegade. So they put him in jail, and then deported him.

There were all sorts of strange romance in that Reverend Abbot Jochao Choa-Kung—British politics, the adventures of a war spy, Far Eastern intrigue, a weird assortment of religious affairs, and quantities of hokum.

THERE WERE TWO HUNGARIAN BROTHERS WHO FOR YEARS were enemies. They were noblemen of the highest rank, and played spectacular parts in affairs of their country. Their historical roles were extreme opposites, and political animosity tore them angrily apart.

Count Joseph and Count Michael Karolyi came of a great Magyar clan dominant in Hungary for centuries. Count Joseph followed stanchly in the ways of his ancestors. He stood at the head of the Monarchist party, leading the ancient aristocracy in its struggle to restore the imperial dynasty on the banks of the Danube. Count Joseph ran true to form, the traditional form of the Karolyis.

Far otherwise was it with Count Michael. He became a Liberal, an extremist. When the monarchy was overthrown at the end of the World War, he joined the revolutionaries and became President of the Hungarian Republic. He did not remain President for long. There was a Bolshevik uprising and aristocratic Count Michael turned the government over to the Communists, who then in the days of Bela Kuhn staged a murderous reign of Red terror.

The Communist regime was speedily overthrown, and Hungary returned to conservative ways. Count Michael fled to Paris. There he remained, impoverished, living in a garret, supported by gifts from friends, and still fighting the battle of radical liberalism.

He was the execration of the noble caste to which he belonged, and the leader of that noble caste was his brother, Count Joseph. There was bitter enmity between them. They held no communication with each other. Each flew into a rage at the mention of his brother's name.

Then at last a reconciliation occurred—a reconciliation from beyond the grave. Count Joseph Karolyi died. The reconciliation was made in his will. In his last testament he wrote: "I beg my brother's pardon if I should have judged him unjustly. It was only because of my greater love for my country than for him. I do not wish to depart from this world with anger in my heart toward anyone."

The will continued with an injunction from Count Joseph to his son, bidding him to strive to have Count Michael's confiscated estates restored.

*
=

A SPY DRAMA IN GERMANY WAS PLAYED OUT TO A DREADFUL and bitter end, with the execution of two German women by the ax. The unhappy victims were Baroness Benita von Berg and Frau Renati von Natzmer, both of the highest social circles. Their trial had been surrounded by the most intense secrecy—the prosecution of a Polish officer and a whole group of German women accused of being his dupes in a gigantic spy game.

The Polish officer, Captain Baron George von Sosnowsky, had been a dazzling social figure in the gay life of Berlin—a glittering host to whose champagne suppers came the highest dignitaries in Germany. He was surrounded by beautiful women, wives and daughters of the rich and the noble. The accusation was that this combined master spy and high-life Prince Charming had used this circle of beauties to gather German military secrets, which he then sold to France—technical secrets about German military airplanes.

When the espionage doings were detected and exposed

by the Gestapo, the German authorities were willing to turn the Baron over to Poland, and exchange him for prominent German spies in prison in Warsaw, but the Baron refused. He insisted on standing loyally by the German women accused with him, and of sharing their fate. Permission was asked of the German Government for him to marry Baroness Benita von Berg, with whom he was connected by ties of long romance. This marriage would have made the woman a Polish subject and thereby rendered her immune from the death penalty; because nations, in times of peace, did not execute spies of foreign nationality. But this romantic salvation did not happen. The German authorities would not sanction the marriage. So the trial before the harsh and relentless People's Court in Berlin went through to the bitter end.

The Polish Baron was sentenced to life imprisonment. For the women who had been his dupes, the story was black. They were of German nationality and were subject to charges not merely of espionage, but also of high treason. The lesser figures among them were sentenced to prison, the two most prominent sentenced to death. There was an appeal to Hitler himself, asking him to ameliorate the supreme penalty. But Hitler took no action.

So now a terrible scene was enacted in a Berlin prison courtyard, as the two executions were carried out in medieval fashion with an executioner's battle-ax wielded by a headsman in a frock coat and silk hat.

Why was the Berlin Government so ruthless and relentless in this punishment of women? The reason was to be found in the intimate military angles that appeared in the case. The first tip leading to the exposé of the spy plot came through the worry of the mother of a girl employed as secretary in the offices of the Reichswehr, Germany's official army. The mother was bothered by the way her daughter had to work every night, all sorts of hours. Also the daughter acquired a rather unexpected fur coat. The mother inquired at the Reichswehr office about why the girl had to work so unmercifully late every night. This led to the discovery that, instead of working, the girl secretary in the Reichswehr offices was spending her nights at the parties of the social lion, Baron Sosnowsky. That girl was one of the women sent to prison. Another of the prison sentences was inflicted on the daughter of a former German general.

The military aspect came to a climax in the cases of the two women who were executed. Frau von Natzmer had married into the family of the German General von Natzmer, who was killed in the World War. As for Baroness von Berg, who was the Polish Baron's chief partner in the spy plot—her first husband was a nephew of General von Falkenhayn, German chief-of-staff and commander of the Kaiser's army in the early part of the World War.

She was divorced from Falkenhayn's nephew, and became infatuated with Sosnowsky. Trying to break the fascination he exerted over her, she contracted another marriage —with Baron von Berg, who was an engineer, an expert on aviation motors at the great Siemans Motor Manufacturing plant. This connected intimately with the story that the spy ring sold German aviation motor secrets to France. The unfortunate Baroness could not keep away from Sosnowsky. Her second husband was devotedly attached to her, but she was soon again in the power of the master spy. Then disaster and tragic nemesis.

*
=

PICTURE OF A MAN MUTTERING IN HIS SLEEP. HE TOSSES uneasily, with dreams and nightmares, and words come from his lips, strange, terrifying words, broken phrases, fragments of a set speech. In his troubled slumber the man reverts again and again to these words: "My name is Lang. I am the government executioner. These are my assistants. I am very sorry you must hang. You will have a few minutes in which to make a last request."

In that way, talking in his sleep, the government hangman in Austria went out of his head. Official explanation was that he had a nervous breakdown—from overwork. The overwork consisted of the numerous hangings of Socialists and Nazis after the revolutionary outbreaks in Austria. He got thirty-three dollars and fifty cents for a hanging, which he divided with two assistants. The business was lucrative, but it drove him crazy.

Johann Lang was known as Europe's best-dressed executioner. He always wore formal dress, evening clothes, when officiating at the gallows. He was most formal, with a never-changing ceremony, when he went to a condemned man's cell. He had a set courteous speech—that same speech which he later mumbled in his haunted dreams:

"My name is Lang. I am the government executioner. These are my assistants. I am very sorry you must hang. You will have a few minutes in which to make a last request."

IN PARIS THEY GUILLOTINED A KILLER, AND THE EXECUtioner said, "Never again!" That was his last one. Why? Nothing special. He had been intending for some time to retire—retire to his perfumes. He had been planning to quit his grim profession and devote himself to his delicate blends of violets and roses. Because the executioner of Paris was also a dealer in perfumes.

Anatole Deibler inherited his terrifying official job. It had been in his family for three generations. The Deiblers obtained the guillotine franchise from the Sanson family, which had held it for seven generations. It was a Sanson who presided at the guillotine during the Reign of Terror in the French Revolution. But the last of the Sansons turned out to be a no-good fellow, a waster, a spendthrift. He disgraced his profession. He was reputed to have pawned the guillotine, and the government had to get it out of hock.

So he sold the franchise of death to the Deiblers. Anatole Deibler was the son of an executioner and the grand-nephew of an executioner.

In his youth he was a brilliant student, who excelled in Latin. He fell in love with a beautiful girl, and didn't dare tell her who his father was—his father's trade. They were thinking of marriage, when the girl found out. She told Anatole, and a feeling of despair swept over him.

"Yes," said the young lady, "I know who your father is. Don't you think, Anatole, it's about time for you to select a profession? Why don't you take up your father's profession?"

So Anatole did, and married his loved one.

He found that all his time was not occupied, and took up another business on the side. He chose perfumery. He had the soul of an artist, that executioner of Paris. He did exceedingly well, creating new savors of flowery fragrance. Once he almost made a serious error. A friend—and what a friend!—suggested a voluptuous name for the latest Deibler perfume, a rare and enchanting scent, and advised him to call it "A kiss on the neck." The master of the guillotine didn't see the joke. He followed the advice. Luckily, some other friend tipped him off before it was too late, and before Paris had been thrown into a wild howl of laughter. So Deibler changed the name of the perfume and called it "Paradise," rather an apt name, too.

He made more from his perfumes than from his deadly profession, and he said he was a business man. So his retirement from the guillotine was strictly a matter of business. The fastidious, dignified, white-bearded little man of seventy, put on his frock coat and silk hat, sprayed himself with "Paradise," and conducted his two hundred and sixtieth execution. His last one—because there was more profit in perfume.

IN THE OLD CITY OF ARRIS IN FRANCE, THERE WERE NOT enough funerals. So the undertaker committed suicide. He explained with that famous French logic: "I cannot kill people to make funerals. So I will kill myself. There will be at least one funeral."

ENGLAND STAGED A GLITTERING LAW-COURT PAGEANT. A peer of the realm was tried, and they put the show on with all the theatrical color and circumstance required by ancient custom. The Magna Charta, which the barons extorted from King John in the year 1215, decreed that a man must be tried by a jury of his peers. The defendant was Baron de Clifford, whose title dated back to 1299. So a jury of his lordship's peers could only be the House of Peers itself.

It was true that Baron de Clifford was quite a modern person. He achieved an up-to-date sort of fame by marrying

[143]

a daughter of the queen of the London night clubs. The Kit Kat night club queen was a flaunting figure in the gay world of dining, wining and dancing. So when her fair daughter was wedded to that ancient title going back to the year 1299, it made quite a stir—especially when His Lordship was promptly haled into court and fined two hundred and fifty dollars for having falsified his age in the marriage certificate. He was only nineteen, but swore he was twenty-two.

The charge on which he was tried by the House of Peers was hardly of the antique Magna Charta variety. It was based on reckless driving, speeding on the wrong side of the road. There was a crash, a man killed, and Baron de Clifford charged with manslaughter.

The Peers assembled as "The Court of Our Lord the King in Parliament." They were garbed in scarlet robes, trimmed with gold and ermine. On their heads they wore black cocked hats. Viscount Hailsham, the Lord Chancellor, presided in the capacity of Lord High Steward. He sat on a golden throne. The prisoner was ushered in and took his penitent place. Young de Clifford knelt on a velvet cushion.

Then up stepped an official called the "Black Rod." He handed a White Staff to the Lord Chancellor. The White Staff symbolized the trial. Then the barristers, in their full-bottomed wigs, recited the accusation and the defense. The contention of the defense was that it had merely been an unfortunate automobile accident and that there was no real case of manslaughter. As a legal battle the arguments weren't

[144]

so hot. It was the scenery and the stage business that made the show.

When the arguments were complete, an official called the roll, the roll of the peers, the lord spiritual and the lords temporal. He recited the name of each and demanded, "How say you, Lord?" And each peer placed his hand on his heart and said either "Guilty" or "Not Guilty." The verdict was—"Not Guilty," defendant acquitted. Whereupon, Viscount Hailsham, the Lord Chancellor, sitting as Lord High Steward, raised the white wand and broke it across his knee, signifying that the trial was ended.

It was a great show, all according to the ancient Magna Charta won on the Field of Runnymede, and all that remained was to send in the bill. The pageant of trial, with the House of Peers sitting as "The Court of Our Lord the King and Parliament" ran up a cost of fifty thousand dollars. According to law, the cost of trial had to be borne by the county in which the offense was committed. In this case it was the County of Surrey. The people of Surrey had to kick in with the fifty thousand for that traffic case before "The Court of Our Lord the King in Parliament!"

FOR THE FUN OF FIGHTING PARAGUAY IN THE PROTRACTED bitter struggle in the Gran Chaco, it cost Bolivia eight hundred million pesos—a hundred and ninety-five million dollars in American cash. Or rather—it didn't cost Bolivia anything. It was Don Simón Patino who paid the pesos.

But then Don Simón Patino was Bolivia. It was his country in the most literal sense of the word. He just about owned it. He was a fabulous multi-millionaire, recognized to be one of the four or five richest men in the world. And it was he who financed personally the Bolivian part of the Chaco War. He agreed to put up every peso for it. Glad to do it.

The story went back forty years to an obscure mining engineer who made a mistake. He was a small and swarthy Bolivian, and people thought him smart—until he allowed himself to be gypped by taking a bad piece of land for what should have been a good hundred-dollar debt. He did it in behalf of his boss, the man for whom he was working. The land he took for the hundred dollars was so terrible, the boss said "Keep it yourself," and fired him.

The unlucky engineer set out with two Indian guides to see what he could do with this luckless piece of real estate. He found nothing but stone and sand, where even weeds would hardly grow. It wasn't of any possible use—on the surface. So the engineer started to dig—and he struck tin. He discovered a tin mine that in one ten-year period proceeded to yield sixty million dollars.

Such was the beginning of Don Simón Patino, who went on to develop and monopolize the tin mines of Bolivia. And Bolivia means tin. Don Simón was reputed to own two-thirds of the world's resources of that humble but necessary metal. Out of every three tin cans tossed on an ash heap, out of every three tinfoil wrappers torn from a bar of chocolate or a stick of chewing gum, two came from the mines of the Bolivian tin magnate.

The fabulous millionaire lived for a long time with his three daughters, until his last daughter got married. Then he was lonely. So he got himself appointed Bolivian ambassador to Paris, and stayed there. At seventy he was a characteristic figure along the boulevards—the man of tin. He financed a war from Paris. The bill? Two hundred million dollars.

THE QUEEN OF EDEN WAS BACK IN HER PARADISE. THE word came from ex-Governor Gifford Pinchot of Pennsylvania. He had had an encounter with the enchantress of the Galápagos, and was quite overcome by her—not by her charms, but at the point of her pistol.

"That island may be paradise," declared Pennsylvania's former governor, "but its queen is no angel." Who ever heard of an angel threatening to shoot so imminent and stately and elderly a gentleman as Gifford Pinchot, statesman of liberalism?

The queen of Paradise was Baroness de Wagner, who appeared in the news with the finding of two bodies on a small desolate island of the Galápagos group. One was the mortal remains of Alfred Rudolph Lorenz, a German who had been a companion of the queen. He had gone paradise-hunting with the Vienna Baroness and they had taken possession of one of the other islands of the Galápagos, uninhabited, a benign place of tropical woodlands, swarming with fish and birds.

Baroness Eloise Bousquet de Wagner ruled this South Sea haunt, pistol in hand, and called herself the Queen of Eden. Another paradise seeker came along, Robert Phillipson, a merchant of Paris. The Queen took him to be her Prince Consort. Thus deposed, Alfred Rudolph Lorenz, the former royal favorite, tried to make his way back to civilization, but the small boat on which he was voyaging was wrecked on a barren shoal and he died on a desolate island.

Later the Queen of Eden had abandoned her kingdom. The government of Ecuador, which actually owned the Galápagos Islands, intervened, and told the Queen that so far from being a royal monarch she would have to behave herself if she wanted to stay. That made her exceedingly angry, and in a royal huff she and her consort Phillipson sailed away. Still later there were rumors that the slim, blonde and tempestuous Baroness was in France, and that Paris would be her paradise hereafter. But that report was premature, as was indicated by the experience of Gifford Pinchot, ex-governor of Pennsylvania.

Gifford Pinchot, his gray hair blown by the winds of adventure, betook himself from Pennsylvania to Paradise. He found the Baroness very much in Eden and very much its Queen—the wild gal of the Galápagos! Former Governor and Mrs. Pinchot were members of a cruise party. They landed at Post Office Bay on Charles Island in the

[148]

Galápagos. They came to a deserted house, and then they followed a path leading through a tangle of forest. Ex-governor Pinchot was striding in the lead.

Suddenly there was a rustling in the bushes beside him, and a shrill voice called "Stop!" The ex-governor felt something poke into his ribs. It was a dainty pearl-handled revolver held by the steady hand of a woman. She was blonde, rather wildly handsome, and dressed in a gown of the latest fashion—there in the jungle. She stared at him with cold blue eyes, always keeping the pistol pointed at him. "I don't like you," she shrilled. "Go, or I'll shoot you." So the ex-governor of Pennsylvania went. He and his party returned to the shore.

A little later another member of the party, wandering around, met the Queen of Eden, and she seemed to like him a little better. She told him something about her strange kingdom. She said she always had at least two men contending for her favor—paradise hunters who drifted out to the islands where subsistence could be had for the gathering. The Queen of Eden governed her suitors, pistol in hand. She told the member of the Pinchot party that when she got tired of one she'd lock him up in a shack and take another. The ones she locked up she never saw again. She said she supposed they escaped and got away from the island. It was the wildest kind of story. The Baroness from Vienna seemed to be the wildest woman of them all.

HERE IS AN INSTANCE OF THE MELODRAMATIC WAY IN which fate can arrange its tragedies. No amount of ingenious imagination could have created a more theatrical series of events than actually occurred at East Braintree, Massachusetts.

There was a spectacular ship launching—a great thirty-million-dollar aircraft carrier sliding down the ways to the sea. The wife of the Assistant Secretary of the Navy was there to do the christening. The ceremonies included a ritual of the sky. Six bright biplanes of the Naval Reserve took off from near-by Squantum Field and circled over the scene of the launching. They were to signalize the act of christening, by going into a power dive as the bottle of champagne was smashed on the bow of the mighty mother ship of warplanes.

Mrs. Charles Edison, wife of the Assistant Secretary of the Navy, had the bottle in her hand. She cried out: "I christen thee *Wasp*." And she swung the bottle for the foaming crash. At that instant the six gleaming planes were diving in close formation, power diving at tremendous speed, and two of them locked wings. At the speed they were going, the wrench of the shock tore the locked wings to pieces. Both planes plunged to earth. One crashed into the roof of a two-story house and burst into flames, setting the house on fire. A seventy-four-year-old man, alone in the house, was stunned by the impact, and had to be rescued.

A quarter of a mile away, in another house, Mrs. Herbert Bess heard the crash. In alarm, she dashed upstairs to where her two-year-old daughter Beverly was asleep. She was hardly in the bedroom, when the second plane fell crashing onto her house. It took the roof right off, swept it from above the heads of mother and child. Neither was injured. The crashing plane bounced across the street and hit another house, smashed into it, and burst into flames. There, nobody was home. The occupants were attending the launching of the great aircraft carrier, the *Wasp!*

Each of the planes had been manned by a pilot and a mechanic, four men in all. Three died in the crashing machines. One took to his parachute. They found his body in the woods, the parachute half opened.

At the launching of the *Wasp,* crowds were showered by fragments of shattered airplane wings, falling to pieces, carried by high wind. It was the height of melodrama—the air tragedy that attended the launching of the airplane carrier.

THE MELLON FORTUNE WAS ONE OF THE GREATEST IN THE world—eight billion dollars or so. Andrew Mellon, when he became the Secretary of the Treasury, was rated at about five hundred million. Then we had news of another Mellon, a cousin of the former Secretary. He was worth about fifteen cents, but he said he was a billion dollars happy.

He was discovered living on the Unemployment Relief Dole, amid the tin-can alleys of the Pittsburgh tenement district. He didn't want his fabulously wealthy cousin to know about it, but the name of William Andrew Mellon on the relief rolls let the story out. So the billion-dollar Mellon went hurrying to the aid of the fifteen-cent Mellon, and the fifteen-cent Mellon accepted just enough aid to buy himself home-cooked dinners from the lady who lived next door.

He wouldn't move out of Tin Can Alley. He said he didn't care if the rest of the Mellon family floated on an ocean of banknotes, with regiments of assorted chefs, chauffeurs and butlers. He was content with his fifteen cents and his happiness. He'd still cook his own breakfast, and wouldn't trade his dingy hall room for the presidential suite at the William Penn.

"It may be just a dump, here where I live," he philosophized, "but I need this place, because I can read, study, think and dream here." He used to have money, a lot of it, but lost it in the Far West. Having lost, he gained. He gained squalor, destitution, a dollar and a half a week out of the public dole—and happiness.

IN CHICAGO SAMUEL INSULL, ONCE THE FABULOUS MILlionaire, took the stand in his own defense. He testified, hoping to save himself from prison. He broke down and wept. In his day he was the stern cold master of a Midwestern utilities empire. At his trial he was an old man in tears—remembering, remembering things of so long ago, recalling scenes that choked his voice with sobs. What was it that made him break down on the witness stand? What was he saying that affected him so much that he couldn't say it any longer, for tears and weeping?

He was telling of his youth—the youth of a lad born in the poorest quarters of London, with little education, no advantages. At fourteen he went to work as an office boy. He studied shorthand and typewriting at night. When he was nineteen he got a job in the London office of Thomas Edison when Edison was expanding in the first flush of his success as the greatest of inventors.

On the American side of the water the wizard of electricity noticed the letters and papers from the London office. He was impressed with the neat typing, the trim and accurate work. He inquired, and brought the young English stenographer to the United States and made him his private secretary.

Samuel Insull told of those events of fifty-three years past—his first impression of Edison, the great inventor's kindness to him, a penniless stenographer, a homesick immigrant boy. He worshiped Edison, and while he recalled the distant memory of his great benefactor, Samuel Insull broke down and cried.

"I'm sorry," he apologized brokenly to judge and jury, "I can't help it."

And judge and jury gazed in amazement at the tears of the former proud lord of millions, now aged, broken, and on his way to prison for the financial collapse that ruined him and impoverished thousands of others.

The final solution of a myth was accomplished at Los Angeles—the bursting of a bubble. A verdict was handed down in a lawsuit against Death Valley Scotty— that singular veteran of the desert who for many years was a legend of fabulous wealth. Gold and gold mines, the rich strike, the big bonanza—all these were attributed to Death Valley Scotty, and admitted by him. He told glowing tales of his gold mines in Death Valley. He scattered money like a drunken miner who has struck a million, and lived in an incredible castle built at huge expense.

In the trial at Los Angeles, testimony revealed that Scotty's money was derived from a rich Chicago insurance man, who had been induced to finance the fantastic tall talker of the desert. The Chicagoan owned the fabulous castle.

The judge, in handing down a verdict, officially called Death Valley Scotty "a fraud and a cheat." His gold mines, his secrets of treasure—"just a pack of lies."

The suit was brought by a man who forty years ago staked Scotty to ten thousand dollars—this on the strength of the mysterious gold mines in Death Valley. The court awarded him all of Scotty's assets—the value of which was exactly nothing. The plaintiff was given title to seventeen

[154]

mining claims in Death Valley, claims which the judge said were worthless. All of which officially exploded the legends of Death Valley Scotty and his tales of secret gold. But I'll bet they'll never die.

*
=

ONE OF THE MOST IMPUDENT HOAXES EVER ATTEMPTED was an aftermath of the tragedy of Amelia Earhart, the famous aviatrix who was lost in the Pacific on a flight around the world. A man went to George Palmer Putnam, husband of Amelia Earhart, and told him that his wife was alive. Not only that, he declared that Amelia Earhart was in the neighborhood of New York.

With this astonishing beginning, the story-teller proceeded to relate a yarn even more astonishing. He said he was a sailor, a member of the crew of a gun-running ship of the South Seas. The gun runner, he continued, while navigating in New Guinea waters, came upon an island where its crew found the wreck of an airplane. Near by was the body of a man killed in the crash and a woman alive, survivor, castaway, Amelia Earhart. The gun runner rescued her, and sailed to America. The ship was lying off the coast near New York, with Amelia Earhart aboard.

The sailor explained that he, as one of the crew, had been commissioned to carry the tidings to the husband of the lost flier. Not only the tidings, but also the proof. He produced a scarf, a brown and white neckpiece—Amelia Earhart's scarf, he said. The most surprising thing of all came when the scarf was identified. A woman secretary of Miss Earhart's recognized it. "Yes," said she, "that brown and white scarf was an article of apparel the aviatrix had owned." Which surely added the strange touch of authenticity to the sailor's story.

The authenticity was diminished when the inevitable demand came—money. The sailor said he wanted two thousand dollars for the return of Amelia Earhart. He had been commissioned by the crew of the gun runner to get the cash. They were a bad lot. "The boat," said he, "has a lot of cutthroats aboard and they talked about dumping your wife into the sea." That was the sinister touch in the demand for the money.

A trap was sprung. Money was given to the sailor with the melodramatic story, whereupon he was arrested by the G-Men. They found him to be a resident of Brooklyn. A sailor? Well—an ex-sailor, very much *ex*. He hadn't been to sea for twenty-two years. He had been living in the Brooklyn neighborhood during all the time of his supposed voyage with the gun runner.

But what about the scarf, that telling piece of evidence which was identified? The ex-sailor broke down and confessed. It was Amelia Earhart's brown and white scarf all right. She had dropped it at Roosevelt Field three years before, when landing from an ordinary flight. The ex-sailor had picked it up and kept it as a souvenir. And souvenir it

[156]

had remained until the sky tragedy of the Pacific. Then the scarf gave the ex-sailor the idea of using it as the basis of his crazy yarn—and the attempt to extort two thousand dollars.

＊
＝

I HEARD A TRAGIC STORY, AS MUCH OF A CLASSIC AS THE OLD one about the soldier who has served in the wars unscathed for many a year, and then falls down his own doorsteps and is killed. I heard the story—and also saw it. We were looking at pictures in the Movietone studio, pictures of a plane skimming the wildest of jungles, diving into tropical canyons, landing on the narrowest and most winding of equatorial rivers. They were Martin Johnson pictures of aviation and wild animal filming in remote unexplored places, the last pictures that Martin Johnson ever made. He had just finished working on them in the motion-picture studio when he went off on a lecture tour and was killed in an airplane accident in California.

Martin and his wife Osa specialized in travel to wild places by plane. He was a pioneer in exploration by the sky route. He brought back a series of great animal pictures, one after another—thrills for all the world. His last one was an epic of wild beasts in Borneo.

They made it with daring flights over the country of head hunters and with landings in a few square yards of log-filled river. Martin's crack aviator, Jim Laneri, had knocked out a giant orang-outang while they were filming and capturing the monster.

I sat with film editor Truman Talley while they ran off the last Martin Johnson picture, and saw as perilous a brand of aviation as I ever looked at—adventure flying to the nth degree. Then comedian and film editor Lew Lehr told me the irony of the Martin Johnson tragedy.

For years Martin Johnson, in his aviation enthusiasm, never would ride on a railroad train if he could help it. He always preferred a plane. But that wasn't the case when he started out on the ill-starred tour to give some lectures. He told Lew Lehr he felt a premonition about flying. He and Osa were not going to take a plane this time. He seemed to feel that they had dared death dangerously enough in their Borneo sky travels—jungles, head hunters, no fit landing places. It was time to call a halt, to knock on wood.

So Martin and Osa took the railroad, much as they disliked the train. Four days to Salt Lake City in a Pullman, much as Pullmans always irked him. But at Salt Lake City he found that his lecture dates on the coast were such that they couldn't possibly make connections by train. They must fly, premonition or no premonition. So Martin and Osa took the plane for Los Angeles.

Then the crash in the mountains in California. Osa gravely injured, Martin killed. He had had a lifetime of hazards in remote places since he first went avoyaging with Jack London twenty-five years before. He was just back from the most dangerous of flying in Borneo, when fate caught up with him in a routine flight on a standard American airline.

THE STORY OF TWO HUMAN BEINGS CAME TO AN END—A drama of blackness. Yes, the blackest of the black, blindness, the absence of all light. One of the world's most renowned women was Helen Keller, that prodigy who lived and became famous—without sight or sound. But Helen Keller had another self, another half. Many years ago Mark Twain wrote to her: "You're a wonderful creature, you and your other half together—Miss Sullivan, I mean."

Anne Sullivan was born at Feeding Hills, Massachusetts, in poverty, in affliction. She was half blind. Her mother died and she went over the hill to the poorhouse. Then, at the Perkins Institute for the Blind, a brilliant operation restored her sight. Thereafter she devoted herself to the care of the blind. Meanwhile, down south a baby was born, a girl destined after early childhood never to see or speak or hear—Helen Keller. She came under the care of Anne Sullivan. In two weeks Anne taught her thirty words, spelling them by touching the hand. Under this tuition, Helen Keller rose to renown. Teacher and pupil remained inseparable for forty-nine years.

Time came when misfortune befell Anne Sullivan, who meanwhile had become Mrs. Macy. What misfortune? Imagine the most dramatic thing you can—she became blind.

And now, turn about, fair play. Helen Keller taught her how to overcome the lack of sight. She schooled her former teacher as devotedly as she herself had been schooled.

Finally Helen Keller stood at the deathbed of her other half. When it was all over, she said: "I pray for strength to endure the silent dark until she smiles upon me again."

A story of shadows, a drama of the dark!

ARMY INTELLIGENCE OFFICERS AND SPECIAL AGENTS OF the Department of Justice conducted an investigation aboard a United States Army transport at San Francisco, but failed to solve the mystery into which they were prying. Perhaps they should have consulted the natives of a remote island in the Hawaiian group. Those primitive Polynesians could have given them the answer. It was a moody thing that a death mystery on shipboard had to occur on the United States transport that was conveying the remains of Father Damien. What a legend surrounded that Belgian priest who made himself the humble friend of the lepers of the South Seas!

He was a young man when he took himself to the leper colony on the Hawaiian island of Molokai, and devoted himself to the care of the sufferers. He stayed there until the end of his life, until he himself contracted the dread malady and died of it. Robert Louis Stevenson immortalized him as "The Martyr of Molokai." In London the Damien Institute was dedicated to his memory, a foundation for research into the nature and cure of that terrifying ill so long a nightmare to humanity.

They were taking the earthly remains of Father Damien back to his native Belgium, where the religious order to which he belonged was beginning the procedure for having him canonized as a saint—Saint Damien of Molokai. The United States Government lent its aid at the personal request of King Leopold of Belgium, who asked Washington to help in returning the body of the leper priest. That's why the remains were aboard a United States Army transport.

The mystery at sea was the disappearance of the captain of the transport. Captain E. S. McLellon either was a suicide or he accidentally fell overboard. What the investigation learned by repeated questioning was simple and mystifying. The night before the transport reached the American coast, Captain McLellon retired to his bunk, leaving the command that he should be awakened when the ship came to the seven-mile mark off land. The command was obeyed. Seven miles off shore they went to awaken the captain, but his cabin was empty. He had vanished.

No, neither the Naval Intelligence nor the Department of Justice could find any explanation, but if they had gone to Molokai, the natives in their grass huts would have solved the mystery in their own fashion. They'd have said it was a curse, a curse for disturbing the saint. The legendary Father Damien was regarded as a mighty wonder-working spirit by the superstitious primitives of those parts, and they'd have said: "The curse struck at the Number One Man of the ship that was taking him away from his brother lepers of Molokai."

ONE OF THE GREATEST OF AMERICAN TACKLES, JOE SUL-livan of Notre Dame, died and was mourned by his father, Police Lieutenant Tim Sullivan. Nor was Joe forgotten at Notre Dame. Came the great game against Ohio State, and sitting at his radio in his Long Island home that afternoon was the gray-haired police veteran, Tim Sullivan. In the first half the Ohio State men crossed the Notre Dame line for two touchdowns. When they scored the second, Tim Sullivan looked up, sighed, and said: "Mother, how beau-tiful it would be if our Joe could go in out there."

What Tim didn't know was that between halves Coach Elmer Layden was in the locker room with the Notre Dame team. He wasn't bawling the Irish out for being scored on twice. He just looked at them and said: "Don't forget, boys, we're doing this for Joe. This is Joe's game." And it was Joe's game. With that burning thought, the fighting Irish rushed out on the field and plucked victory out of defeat in the most dramatic ball game of that year or almost any year.

Back in the home on Long Island, as the feverish words of the announcer came tumbling out of the radio, Lieutenant Tim Sullivan listened with rising excitement. Galloping sentences described the irresistible rush of the Irish. And the police veteran could be heard gasping: "By gorry, Joe, if you could only hear that!"

When the final whistle blew, he cried: "They've won, Mother; they've won, Joe!" And with those words he slid gently off the chair to the floor. The heart that had carried him through many years of police work had given way under the excitement. He died.

The doctors said it was "arterial hemorrhage." What actually happened was that Joe Sullivan's father had gone to join his boy.

IN THE STRANGE SAGA OF FATHER DIVINE, THE MOST UProarious event was staged in front of police headquarters in New York. It was the weirdest kind of hullabaloo. Wild yells of "Peace!" and "God!" Milling throngs of blacks singing and chanting strange hallelujahs! Frenzied anthems like this: "We'll always go on. Father Divine is God Almighty! We'll always go on." This furore accompanied the jailing, arraignment and release on bail of the Negro cult leader who was worshiped by thousands of fanatical followers.

The self-styled deity made some interesting comment about his arrest, which occurred at Milford, Connecticut. The police had a tip that Father Divine was hiding in a cult resort there, one of those haunts of religious uproar which he calls "heaven." When the cops arrived at the gate of heaven, they were confronted by a giant Negro, who said he was Simon Peter. And Peter refused them admission into heaven. The cops pushed the saint-with-the-key around a bit and searched the building.

They found "God" in the cellar, hiding behind the furnace. It was a critical moment for the dusky deity, as he explained later. He said he tried to "invisibilize" himself, but it didn't work. His divine powers failed him when the cops looked that way, and he remained entirely visible as they nabbed him. He was whisked to New York, to police headquarters, and locked up for the night, his case to be heard in the morning.

The news flashed to the dusky corners of Harlem, and during the night thousands of "God's angels" flocked downtown to police headquarters. They jammed the streets around that formidable building, pushing, swarming, parading, with shouts of "Peace!" and "God!" The whole neighborhood re-echoed with their frantic chanting. "Let not your hearts be troubled," they sang—"we're not afraid. Father Divine is ruler of this whole round world!" The leader appeared to be a shouting angel called "Happy Heart."

They kept up the pandemonium all night long, and in the wee hours got hungry, swarmed into a near-by lunch room, and ate up everything. One dark angel thought of the divinity in his prison cell—he might be hungry. The angel procured a huge stack of egg sandwiches and took them to the door of the jail. "God's favorite food is eggs," said the angel.

In the morning Father Divine went through the formalities of the law. He appeared guarded by two Negro detectives, and they made a strange-looking trio. Cops are big fellows, and the two Negro detectives were giants. The cult leader was short, squat, pudgy and yellow. The Harlem deity seemed all the more insignificant between the two towering Goliaths.

The cause of the arrest was a stabbing affray which had occurred at the Harlem heaven. Questioned by the police and the judge, Father Divine pleaded innocent. He declared he hadn't anything to do with the knifing of a white man who tried to serve a court summons on him at some celestial proceedings. "I was preaching with great enthusiasm," he testified. "Someone started to push me around. And there was some excitement." That, he said, was all he knew about the stabbing.

He was held on five hundred dollars bail, whereupon in the courtroom a Negro woman in a red dress pushed forward. From her purse she drew a huge roll of bills, peeled off one hundred five-dollar notes, and handed them to the clerk—the bail money. She turned to the dusky divinity with humble reverence: "I'm Saint Mary Bloom," she said. "I'm one of your angels."

Word flashed to the crowd outside, and the yell went up: "God is free, God is free!" The fat little divinity emerged amid wild shrieking, and started uptown in a shiny limousine. He went to his Harlem heaven, and there

[165]

another milling mob was gathered. A bedlam of jubilee was staged, with the chant, "God is reigning in the land!"

The pudgy divinity was in his glory, but the police said they had found something else against him—concerning bootleg coal. They alleged that the Divine heaven in Harlem was being heated with illegal fuel—provided by an angel called the Blessed Thomas. This angelic creature scorned the bootleg coal charge. "God don't need earthly fuel," explained the Blessed Thomas.

More important still was the apostasy of "Faithful Mary." The Divine custom was to hold extensive properties in the name of various angels. A large part of the real estate was in the name of Faithful Mary, but she renounced her former "God" and declared that she wouldn't turn the property over to him. That was bad.

But the climax of the heavenly troubles came in an announcement made by Mother Horne. The Mother ran an opposition cult in Harlem, a rival of the dusky "God." She proclaimed that she was going to preach a sermon about Father Divine—a real stem-winder. Her text would be: "The Devil's Got to Move On." When "God" is called "Old Nick," that's real trouble.

The names that Father Divine's angels gave themselves were a frequent source of comedy. Occasionally, there'd be a tangle in court when they'd insist on their heavenly monickers being put on record, to the astonishment and bewilderment of judges and other legal functionaries. The funniest instance occurred in the case of Jeannette Bourne. She was a forty-year-old Negress, a native of the West Indies, a British citizen. No one could excel her fervor when she uttered: "Peace, it's wonderful!" And of course she had adopted a heavenly name.

She applied for American citizenship, and in court was asked the routine question, "What's your name?"

To which she answered: "My name is Love Nut."

"What?" demanded the astounded judge.

"Love Nut," she repeated; "I'm one of Father Divine's children." And she insisted that she be made an American citizen under that nutty cognomen.

Did the judge utter "Peace, it's wonderful"? He did not. His Honor said: "I think you're crazy. Citizenship denied."

So Love Nut had to go on being an angel of British citizenship.

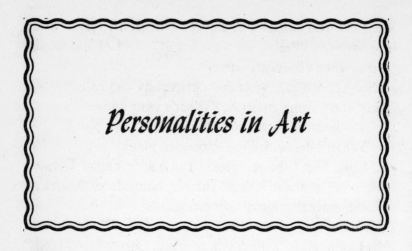

Personalities in Art

F̲ROM symphony to cinema, from poet to tap dancer, the realm of the esthetic and entertaining has always abounded in the flare of personality. Artistic temperament, they say tritely. There is something vivid in the sensibilities and high-pressured fancies of music or verse or stage playing that makes for the larger vagaries and spacious extremes. Perhaps the people in art, by going to folly more, arrive at more wisdom. Anyway, it's quite a pageant of personalities.

THERE WAS OPERA, ROMANCE AND A BIT OF SCANDAL AT La Scala in Milan. The scandal part of it pertained to the government of Mussolini. As a matter of music, the occasion witnessed the production of a new opera by the world-renowned composer, Mascagni. The romance was the story of a seventy-one-year-old musician who in his early youth scored a fabulous success, and then dwindled into a comparative failure.

Mascagni wrote *Cavalleria Rusticana* in eighteen-ninety, and it instantly swept the musical world. Its popularity has never diminished. Mascagni was the toast of the realm of music. He went to London to conduct *Cavalleria* and received tremendous glory and ballyhoo. He got a salary of ten thousand dollars a week. He took with him seventy-five dress shirts and a hundred and seventy-six collars. Yes, the composer of *Cavalleria* was riding high.

He proceeded to write one opera after another, but he never could repeat. Musically they were good, but they never caught on. For forty-five years Mascagni tried to duplicate that triumph of his youth, but he never succeeded.

Then, in his old age, he wrote another opera, *Nero*, based on that sinister figure of Imperial Rome. The première at La Scala, in Milan, was one of the most brilliant of musical and social events. Seats in even the topmost gallery were twelve dollars each. People in boxes paid a hundred and fifteen dollars a seat. Tremendous prices anywhere, and especially in Italy. All was set for a triumph, and the triumph occurred. The opera scored a first-night ovation.

Now about the scandal. The musical pageant of Rome in the days of the Emperor Nero was in one of its affecting moments. One of the characters on the stage declaimed a tragic phrase. "Rome is starving," he sang; "there is no bread!"

To which a loud voice from the Milanese peanut gallery responded with a yell: "That's nothing new. The same condition still exists!"

Did that cause consternation! It was a slap at Mussolini and the Fascist regime. The police instantly went in search of the disturber.

In spite of that small somber note, the première of Mascagni's new opera *Nero* scored a tremendous first-night triumph. But the success was mostly a matter of first night. *Nero*, too, failed to catch on—was no *Cavalleria Rusticana.*

ANOTHER TOSCANINI STORY TO BE ADDED TO THE LIBRARY of anecdotes about the famous maestro. With an N.B.C. orchestra he toured South America, giving a series of concerts. At Montevideo Toscanini suddenly sent out an urgent and unexpected rehearsal call. The musicians were surprised. There seemed no reason for this special rehearsal, and the day for which it was called was the Fourth of July.

They assembled in the orchestra pit of the empty theater. Toscanini took his place at the conductor's stand, and said: "You are from the United States. This is the Fourth of July, and I think it is an occasion which should be celebrated. I have called you together—only to play the 'Star-Spangled Banner.' "

Whereupon he led them through a thrilling performance of the National Anthem—in an empty theater at Montevideo.

A SPIRIT OF TRAGIC IRONY HOVERED OVER A DEATHBED IN Paris. One of the great figures of the arts was taking leave of the world, one of the most famous of names—Chaliapin, the legend-crowned Russian basso.

He was a fabulous figure of music, a Russian peasant reared in sordid poverty. His inspired gifts of voice and art carried him to a height of fortune and renown as the greatest operatic basso of his time. At his peak his earnings were a quarter of a million dollars a year. And he strutted his part—the Russian peasant raised to the topmost pinnacle—the Volga Boatman, King of Song.

He was a giant of a man, six feet four, as I knew him, built like one of those Russian wrestlers, huge shoulders, ponderous muscle, the figure of a professional strong-man. And he was proud of his great stature and bulk. He used to swagger like a hulking Goliath.

His appetite was stupendous, and so was his thirst. He'd eat enough for three men. Before breakfast he'd have a snack—a huge bowl of raw chopped cabbage, raw onions and slices of black bread, a reminder of his Russian peasant origin. And he'd drink his fiery native vodka by the gallon, it seemed. He was known to put famous tipplers under the

[171]

table. Chaliapin drinking on, roaring with song! His love affairs were of similar ample dimensions: many adventures, many children.

Such was Chaliapin, a Gargantua of art. Of what malady did he die? That's the irony—anemia! You've seen anemic people, thin, pale, wraith-like. The utter and complete reverse was bulky, burly Chaliapin. And yet, in his last years, he was taken with pernicious anemia. His giant frame and mighty appetite simply wasted away. A Gargantua—fallen away to a shadow. Mockery!

But there was nothing contradictory about Chaliapin's last moments. Napoleon died thinking in his delirium he was commanding a great battle. And Chaliapin died with a delusion of singing an opera.

He lay mumbling feverish, broken phrases, and they heard him say: "What theater am I in?" And then his last words: "I can't sing here." No, he could never sing here again. Chaliapin might voice a melody in some other realm, singing *Boris Godunof*—somewhere beyond the stars.

IT WAS TIME TO TELL STORIES ABOUT ANTONIO SCOTTI. HE was dead—at seventy-one. Scotti, the baritone, who for so many years trod the stage in the glory of New York's Metropolitan Opera House. He became a legend, specializing in dark and sinister operatic characters. He was surrounded by a wealth of anecdote, one of those people whose requiem might be: "Tell a story about him." So on the radio I talked about the furniture in *La Tosca*.

The anecdote went back to the days when Scotti and Jeritza played hair-raising drama in that somber old thriller of music. I had the story from Carlo Edwards, long an assistant conductor at the Met. He related that Scotti was always finicky about the furniture on the stage in *La Tosca*. Always before the second act he would go on the stage and carefully arrange the chairs, table and couch—to suit. But Jeritza, the soprano, had her own notions. She wanted to have the furniture her own way, and she would only have to wait.

For Scotti had one invariable custom. Just before strutting on the stage to sing, he would go to his dressing room and kiss his mother's picture. It was a superstition with him. Jeritza would wait until he had gone to pay his devotions to the maternal photograph, then she would rearrange the furniture to please herself. By the time Scotti got back, the act was about to begin, and there was nothing he could do. The furniture stayed as she had fixed it.

To his last moment the great Scotti upheld his reputation as a man about whom stories were to be told. He died in Naples, but his death was kept secret. It was a headline, but Scotti wanted no headlines. It was his wish that the news of his passing should be broken in the humblest way —by a bought-and-paid-for notice of a few lines in the obituary column of a Neapolitan newspaper. That appeared—a last gesture of humility.

*
=

THE GREAT CONTRALTO, MADAME SCHUMANN-HEINK, AS nearly everybody knows, was one of the tragic figures of the World War. She had sons serving on both sides, in the American Army and in the German Army, and also in the German submarines—brothers fighting brothers. On the battlefield one of the famous singer's sons, who was an American lieutenant, ran across a bunch of German prisoners one day. They had just been brought in, and were in bad shape—wounded, exhausted, hungry, covered with mud, in tatters. One of them turned to Schumann-Heink's son and asked for a cigarette.

"I haven't a cigarette," replied the American lieutenant, "but perhaps you would like a cigar." And he handed the woebegone German a first-rate Havana that had been sent from the States.

The German's eyes bulged as he took the cigar. He started to smoke it, and a radiant expression came over his face. The wartime cigars in Germany were something frightful—usually cabbage or something of the sort. The prisoner, as he smoked away, pulled a handsome watch out of his pocket and handed it to the son of Schumann-Heink.

[174]

Then he turned, and quickly got under way with the other prisoners.

Years passed. Schumann-Heink's son became a second officer on a ship, and one day was strolling along the streets of Hamburg. A man dashed up to him. It was the same prisoner.

"Have you still got my watch?" he exclaimed.

"Yes, here it is."

The German took the watch, looked at it, almost fondled it. That timepiece had been a precious keepsake for him. Schumann-Heink's son wanted to give it back to him.

"No," cried the German. "I merely want to look at it once more. It is yours now—fair exchange. That cigar was worth more than a wagon load of watches."

He handed the watch back, turned on his heel, and vanished in the crowd.

AT BOSTON AN AGED WOMAN LAY ILL. SHE WAS EIGHTY-ONE and without money, yet she was the composer of one of the most famous bits of music on this earth. When her plight became known, the American Society of Composers, Authors and Publishers came to her rescue with money to provide her with a private hospital room and a private nurse. They did this in acknowledgement of her contribution to American music.

She was Mrs. Effie Canning Carlton. Do you recognize the name? What song did she write? Can you guess? Well, many a long year ago, Mrs. Effie Canning Carlton composed "Rock-a-bye Baby."

> Rock-a-bye, baby, on the treetop,
> When the wind blows the cradle will rock;
> When the bough breaks, the cradle will fall,
> Down will come baby, bough, cradle, and all.

On a guess, I'd say that that song has been sung in this land more often than any other—innumerable mothers endlessly crooning "Rock-a-bye, baby, on the treetop." For that most popular of songs, Mrs. Effie Canning Carlton never received even one penny of royalties.

In England, Mrs. Alice Hargreaves died at the age of eighty-two. When she was a little girl, those many years ago, her father was dean of Christ Church at Oxford. In the family were ten children. Three of the girls were of the age when listening to stories is the best. They were Alice, Lorina and Edith.

There was a young Oxford professor of mathematics named Charles Dodgson, who used to row a punt up the river and visit the dean's house, where there were so many children. He particularly liked the three little girls, Alice,

Lorina and Edith, but he liked Alice the best. The girls always used to say, "Tell us a story, please." And Alice would add: "And please make it a story with some nonsense in it." That's why the professor of mathematics liked Alice the best.

So one historic summer afternoon he told Alice a story with very much nonsense in it. He made it up as he talked —about a little girl named Alice who fell down a rabbit hole. There was a White Rabbit, an Ugly Duchess, a Mad Hatter and a March Hare, Tweedledum and Tweedledee, the Walrus and the Carpenter. Later he wrote it down, and published it. He signed it with the pseudonym of Lewis Carrol, and called it *The Adventures of Alice in Wonderland*.

That Mrs. Hargreaves who died in England was the little girl in the story, the original Alice. Let's believe that Alice went to Wonderland.

GEORGE BERNARD SHAW WAS STILL CONTRIBUTING TO THE gaiety of nations. G. B. S. was on a round-the-world cruise. Before he boarded the liner he announced publicly that he would not give a single autograph to anybody for any reason or any purpose whatsoever.

Whereupon the ship stewards foresaw a chance of turning an honest penny. On some liners it's the custom not to pay cash for drinks, but to sign a check. They thought they'd keep all of G. B. S.'s bar checks and sell them to autograph hunters for a nice profit.

Imagine the disgust of those stewards, who evidently were not too well acquainted with literary lore, when they learned that there wouldn't be any bar checks from G. B. S. As any Shavian could have told them, Shaw was a teetotaler—the most notorious vegetarian and teetotaler in the world.

While Shaw was voyaging down the China coast, he received an invitation from the Rotary Club in Shanghai, China, to attend a Rotary luncheon. Shaw curtly said: "No." Asked why he wouldn't go, he answered: "Rotarians always remind me of a bunch of stuffed monkeys all having lunch together."

When the President of the Shanghai Rotary Club was told about the Shavian gibe, he retorted: "Mr. Shaw is quite right. We Rotarians are like a lot of stuffed monkeys. But that's why we asked him to come and have lunch with us. There's always room for one more."

I AM AFRAID THERE'S A LACK OF POETIC SENTIMENT IN THE souls of some United States quarantine officials. They enforce the law, the letter of the law. Okay! But they make no concession to the more lyrical heights of emotion. Take this story of four refugees from Europe, who arrived by ship at New York—a man, a woman, and two birds.

Let us see who the man was. Famous for many years; a legend, so long a legend that one hardly thought of him as being in the land of the living. The Belgian poet, Maurice Maeterlinck—author of *The Bluebird*. Maeterlinck was seventy-seven years old, and he arrived on our shores, a refugee from his conquered native land. With him was his beautiful red-haired wife, Renée, an actress. To say that she was younger than the seventy-seven-year-old poet was to put it mildly.

How about the two birds? Madame Maeterlinck carried them in a cage. What kind of birds? Can there be any doubt? They were bluebirds. Ah, yes, poetic sentiment, indeed. With his lyrical drama, *The Bluebird*, Maeterlinck made worldwide success. So for pets he had a pair of bluebirds.

What had Maeterlinck to say about the war tragedy that had overwhelmed Europe? He was the poet of brightness and joy—the bluebird for happiness. He spoke darkly in these words: "I am stunned. Nothing can be done. All is done. You can't think. What has happened is catastrophic. All you can do is wait. You must wait for history to clarify itself."

He said he lost everything in the Nazi invasion of Belgium. The only possessions he brought with him were his two bluebirds. Yet he had means of livelihood here in America—the royalties on his play, *The Bluebird*.

[179]

To all of which America should have exclaimed, "Welcome, Maurice Maeterlinck, you and your actress wife and your two bluebirds." But no—that was not said.

Along came two quarantine officers with heavy steps, those soulless fellows. They gave a welcome to Maeterlinck and Madame Maeterlinck, but not to the bluebirds. There was a law, there was a regulation, you couldn't bring birds into the country. I suppose it had something to do with the parrot disease or the hoof-and-mouth disease, or something. Those hardhearted quarantine men said "No"; Maeterlinck's bluebirds could not be admitted into the United States.

Alas, the poet sighed sadly, but nothing could soften the quarantine hearts of flint. No bluebirds. So the melancholy Maeterlinck had to dispose of his poetic pets before he could enter the United States. He gave them to the captain of the ship that had brought him over. Alas, poor bluebirds! I think those quarantine men deserved an award, a testimonial—a pair of stuffed buzzards.

In Paris they gave a new play, a comedy called *Bourrachon*, by Louis Doillet. It made a hit.

Well, people spoke of the playwright and the long struggle he had had. Ten years ago he wrote a successful play, but after that his luck seemed to peter out. He couldn't even get a play put on. He was poor and wretched, striving, always striving.

Then at last, after years, the manager accepted his comedy called *Bourrachon*, and, as they say on Broadway, it went over big. It was a wow. That may seem like the perfect ideal of a happy ending, but there's something more to the story—a tragic something more.

The playwright had been in bad health for some time. He grew weaker as the rehearsals of his play went on. The night when it was produced he was sinking. The curtain rose, the actors played their laughing parts in the comedy, but the playwright was dying. At his home he was informed that the play seemed to be going well, but he died before the final curtain and the ovation.

His last words were: "If I die before the end, don't tell the news. I should not like to influence the critics."

The audience shouted and cheered with applause for the play, and the critics wrote eloquent praises, but the playwright can never know anything about that.

A LAWSUIT HAD BROADWAY AGOG. EDDIE CANTOR, THE comedian, sued by Dave Freedman the gag man, sued for a quarter of a million dollars! The trial was expected to provide a flashing comedy of courtroom entertainment, but it ended suddenly.

They had been intimate friends and collaborators—the teller of jokes and the creator of jokes. Eddie Cantor and Dave Freedman first became associated when Eddie read a book that Dave had written. Not long out of school, Freedman produced a volume about the doings and sayings of Mendel Marantz, pictured as a lazy, loafing philosopher of the East Side. The philosophies propounded by Mendel were the sort to catch the eye of Eddie Cantor.

"What's love?" asked Mendel. "It's a cigar. The brighter it burns, the quicker it turns into ashes."

"What's marriage? The ash tray."

It wasn't long before Dave Freedman was writing gags and comic skits for Eddie Cantor. Their association continued for a long time. They were the Damon and Pythias of Broadway, the stage, the radio. Then they had a quarrel—about money matters. They became as implacable enemies as they had been devoted friends. They got into court proceedings—with Freedman suing Cantor for a quarter of a million.

A curious thing about Broadway's Number One Gag Man was his devotion to the abstruse arts of higher calculus and post-Euclidian geometry. He was an enthusiastic member of the Mathematician Society. His trade was humor, his amusement was mathematics. Maybe that's how he figured out the two hundred and fifty thousand dollars.

Court opened in the celebrated Broadway case of Freedman versus Cantor, the second day of the trial. On the bench sat Justice Pecora, that same Ferdinand Pecora who rose to fame as chief inquisitor in the Senate Finance Investigation.

Defendant Eddie Cantor was in court. The chief witness of the day was to be Plaintiff Freedman. Gag Man Dave as a witness of the day was expected to provide some lively comic fireworks. Attorney Samuel Leibowitz appeared for him—that same Leibowitz who made headlines in the case of the Scottsboro Negroes and the Hauptman case.

The attorney addressed the court and asked that the case be closed—declared off. "I am sorry to inform the court," he said, "that the plaintiff has died." Dave Freedman, Number One Gag Man, had fallen victim to a sudden heart attack—at thirty-eight.

"That," said Justice Pecora from the bench, "is a decree of a Court from which there is no appeal." And he dismissed the case.

Eddie Cantor was sitting there, his wide eyes growing wider. "This is a most shocking and distressing thing," he said. "I am sure Dave knew in his heart that I was his friend, and that the day would come when in spite of this lawsuit we would be working together again. This show business is cockeyed," Eddie Cantor reflected sadly. "Today, we are fighting each other, tomorrow we are working together."

But Eddie Cantor and Dave Freedman would never work together again.

HERE'S THE STORY OF A TOUGH GUY. IT BEGINS IN THE MOST gentle and genteel fashion—in a clergyman's family, the household of the Colonial Bishop of Claremont in South Africa. The tough guy was the Bishop's son.

The Boer War came and he enlisted in the Life Guards, though he was only fourteen. Then he went to Canada, prospecting for silver. He went broke, and kept life in his bones by telling lies in a barroom, relating tall stories and passing the hat. He collected enough to get into a poker game and made a killing. He rose to the post of a railroad chief of police. From that to prize fighting. The old record books show that the tough guy had the distinction of fighting a no-decision bout with the mighty Jack Johnson at Vancouver.

The World War, and the tough guy enlisted. He became a captain and campaigned in Mesopotamia. He fought in the capture of Baghdad and was made Provost Marshal of the old town of the *Arabian Nights*. He learned Arabic so well that he qualified as a professional interpreter.

After the Armistice, he returned to prize fighting—at the age of thirty-three. But he found he was all washed up. In his first bout he was slashed to bits, cut to ribbons. But an English film producer saw the fight, and decided the beaten-up tough guy looked so tough, he'd make a movie actor for hard-boiled parts. That led to the flicker film, to Hollywood, to renown as Captain Flagg in *What Price Glory?*—and to the nineteen thirty-five Hollywood award.

Victor McLaglen, of course. He got the prize for the best individual male performance in a picture during that year. The top-ranking movie star, who a few years before had been a washed-out pug, expressed his jubilation this way: "It's like being world's champion for a year."

Could it be that Hollywood was going hard and cynical? Lacking in sweetness and light? It looked that way. Of the two prizes, male and female, one went to the tough guy and the other to the bad girl. What about her? She had had some bad breaks. Maybe that was what made her bad.

She studied classic and interpretative dancing in New England, and somebody offered her a part in a summer production where she could display her artistic talents as a coming Pavlowa or Isadora Duncan. When she reported to the theatrical troupe, with her esthetic costumes and all, she found that somebody had kidded her unmercifully. So she got a job as an usher, and then as a waitress.

She went to Hollywood, had a test, and failed miserably, a complete flop. She was ready to chuck everything, when George Arliss thought she was just the type for a part in the picture, *The Man Who Played God*. From then on, success for the bad girl, culminating with the nineteen thirty-five Hollywood honor for her part in *Of Human Bondage*.

ONE OF UNCLE SAM'S DEPUTY MARSHALS, A REAL TWO-GUN man who used to be a frontier sheriff in the tough days of

Yellowstone County, Montana, was assigned the job of serving a subpoena on Charlie Chaplin. Said the ex-two-gun man: "That ought to be easy."

He drove up to the front door of Charlie's home in Beverly Hills and asked for him. A maid promptly slammed the door in his face. Whereupon he rented a laundry cart, drew up to the rear door, and started up with a bundle. The first person he ran into was the same maid, and she threw him out again.

His next device was the well-worn stratagem of dressing up in a Western Union messenger's uniform and pretending to deliver a letter. He demanded Mr. Chaplin's own signature on the receipt and was told: "The master isn't home." With brilliant originality the deputy borrowed a satchel such as surgeons carry their instruments in. When the butler opened the door, he tried to scurry in, saying he was the doctor that Mr. Chaplin had sent for. To which the butler said: "Sorry, sir, Mr. Chaplin is playing golf."

The deputy learned that Charlie was staging a big party at his home on a Saturday night. So the hardy ex-frontiersman laid aside his ten-gallon hat and his guns and rented him an evening suit, complete down to the ebony cane. In that disguise he had no difficulty in getting into the party. Leaning against the table where the ice-cream sodas were being served, he got chummy with a movie producer. After a few minutes, the deputy said: "By the way, I wish you'd introduce me to my host."

To that the producer replied: "I'd love to, but Charlie isn't here. He's at Palm Springs."

The astonished deputy exclaimed: "You mean he isn't here at his own party?"

The producer replied: "Oh, no; Charlie often gets tired of a party before it begins and runs away somewhere. But that doesn't prevent the party from going on anyway, going on indefinitely."

The deputy never did serve the subpoena.

LUPE VELEZ, THE MEXICAN HOT TAMALE OF HOLLYWOOD, was swindled, just plain gypped. On the screen she was a subtle siren. In other words, a wise dame. But Lupe fell for one of the crudest con-game tricks. It's an old fortune-teller stunt. Many people know how it works. Lupe does—*now*.

A gypsy fortune teller got Lupe into her magical toils and read her palm, foretold her future, and convinced Lupe that she possessed the darkest secrets of gypsy sorcery. Then the fortune teller told the wise and sophisticated screen star about the most wonderful witchcraft of all. She'd bring Lupe all the good luck in the world by performing a cabalistic ceremony over a wad of Lupe's money. That was the most powerful kind of necromancy—blessing the bankroll. The bigger the bankroll, the better.

Lupe believed it, and drew twenty-five hundred dollars out of the bank. This fistful of money she brought to the gypsy for the mystic ritual. The fortune teller went ahead with the complicated incantations of Mumbo Jumbo—the blessing of the bankroll. And somewhere in the process of that occult ceremony, the bankroll disappeared. After which the gypsy herself disappeared.

So Lupe was out twenty-five hundred dollars. And was Lupe mad! Caramba! She virtually did a loop-de-loop. She put in a complaint to the police, and impatiently waited for the fortune teller to be caught. At length came the exciting tidings. The gypsy was under arrest at Evansville, Indiana. Lupe signed the extradition papers to bring her back to Hollywood.

"I'm going to feex her up," she shouted. "Number one—I punch her in the nose. Number two—I kick her in the teeth. Number three—I pull her hair."

That fortune teller needed all the black art of her gypsy tribe to save her nose, her teeth, and her hair.

THE AUCTIONEER'S VOICE RANG OUT, "GOING, GOING, GONE!" in one of the most singular auction sales ever staged. We don't think of the business of knocking things down to the highest bidder as a thing of sentiment and emotion. Though, of course, tears in melodrama have often been shed when they auctioned off the widow's home because she couldn't pay the mortgage—before the hero saves the situation at the last moment. Anyway, there was sentiment and emotion in an auction at North Tarrytown. There was almost a catch in the auctioneer's throat, as he bawled, "What am I offered for this priceless object?" Of course, old leather-lungs really didn't sob at North Tarrytown. Auctioneers aren't that way. But many a furtive tear moistened the cheeks of the spectators and buyers—at the sale under the hammer of the belongings of Elsie Janis.

The former Sweetheart of the A.E.F. was in attendance, beaming with smiles, livening up the proceedings with that Elsie Janis showmanship which delighted a generation of show goers. The favorite entertainer of the doughboys in France was auctioning off all her worldly possessions, her splendid estate and manor house, her collections of valuable articles. Doing it to square with her creditors—and for charity.

The heartthrobs at the Elsie Janis auction can be illustrated by a couple of the bids and bidders. Heartthrob Number One: a silver slipper fit for Cinderella. Presented to Elsie by her fellow actors, when she starred in *The Silver Slipper*. When the gleaming little shoe appeared under the hammer, a man eagerly bid for it and bought it. In his memory lingered a youthful vision, the vision of girlish, sparkling Elsie Janis in *The Silver Slipper*. He had seen the show in nineteen twelve.

Throb Number Two: An oil man from Detroit leaped to purchase a bracelet, a silver box, and a bottle with a silver top. What did these mean to him? The Detroit oil man had been an actor once, and had played in *Elsie Janis and Her Gang*, in nineteen-nineteen. Whenever he had seen the

[189]

star's dressing table, he had noticed that bracelet, that silver box and that silver-topped bottle. Now they brought back to him his days as an actor—the younger days of a Detroit oil man.

And so the bidding continued—going, going, gone.

ONE OF THE FASCINATING THINGS IN THE LIFE OF A NEWS man is the finding of a classic story among the items that flash across the wires. Some classic or other—of tragedy or humor; irony, mockery. Take this one about Mademoiselle Polaire. Remember her, some of you old-timers? She was the rage of the stage years back—no world-famous beauty, she wasn't beautiful at all, rather the reverse. Her interesting homeliness was one of her points; and she had the smallest waist in the world, a notable perfection in the era of tight lacing. Immensely acclaimed as a variety actress, favorite of grand dukes, she amassed a fabulous fortune. She spent it just as fabulously, so it wasn't surprising to hear that at sixty-five she had long since had to leave her gilded haunts, had been compelled to go and live in a poor section of Paris. Familiar, melancholy tale of a once-renowned actress.

What brought Mademoiselle Polaire back in the news? It was an always effective headline—saved by her pet dogs. The old-time actress fell against a glass door, was knocked unconscious and cut severely. She would have bled to death, save for her dogs, which barked and raised an uproar and attracted the attention of the neighbors. So Mademoiselle Polaire was rescued and taken to a hospital.

While the doctors were dressing the wounds of the once-famous star, she wailed and complained. About the pain? About the misfortune of her fall? Not at all. She scolded and berated! Theatrical managers refused to give her contracts any more. That was her moan. "They will not engage me to appear on the stage—me, Mademoiselle Polaire."

＊
＝

Hilburn Lloyd, a Shakespearian actor who played for a number of seasons with Robert Mantell, told me some curious things about the great Thespian. For years, when he was touring up and down America, Mantell never lay down to sleep—not once in years. The man who brought Shakespeare to most of the cities and towns of this country always slept sitting up. And when he went to bed at night, he would sit in bed, smoking his pipe, and wearing his derby hat.

In his later years, when he was suffering terribly from an injured knee, the pain was so great that sometimes he would forget his lines. But he would go right on and mumble his way through. He could actually mumble in Shakespearian meter. The audience would never know the difference and

[191]

would applaud his best mumbles wildly. He got some of his greatest acclaim that way.

ON CHRISTMAS I PICKED UP THE NEW YORK *AMERICAN* and glanced at the headline of the column called "Today," so familiar in the Hearst newspapers. Arthur Brisbane's column. I read the first paragraph, a Christmas sentiment characteristic of Brisbane the optimist: "Another Christmas has come," it read, "a birthday that means kindness and hope for many millions of human beings."

Yes, hope for millions—but that particular Christmas required more than mere human and earthly hope for Arthur Brisbane. A few hours later came the flash—Brisbane had died. The almost legendary figure of American journalism expired on Christmas Day in his New York apartment, in a lofty skyscraper far above Manhattan Island whose glories he had so oft extolled.

He lived a great life. His father was a famous figure of his time, one of the earliest pioneers of socialism in the United States. His son inherited a concern for human welfare. He came to prominence in the fabulous newspaper days of Joseph Pulitzer, when editors battled mightily for causes. He was one of Pulitzer's brilliant young stalwarts. Then William Randolph Hearst made his own slashing entrance into American journalism. Opposing Pulitzer, he took from his rival a whole staff of able men headed by Arthur Brisbane. As editor of the New York *Evening Journal* Brisbane rose to great wealth. His salary was reputed to be a quarter of a million a year, on top of which he made a fortune in real-estate investments. Becoming the author of the immensely successful column, "Today," he ranked as the dean and most successful of American journalists.

I saw him often at public affairs—national conventions and such. He always sat in the press section among the other newspapermen, his typewriter in front of him, and he pecked away as industriously as the most hard-working of the young reporters. It seemed to be a point of pride with him, at the height of career and success, to play the part simply of the reporter, the working newspaperman—until finally for Arthur Brisbane this earthly today has become that other tomorrow.

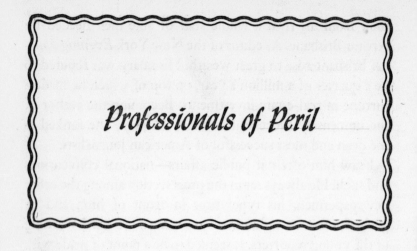

Professionals of Peril

IN the Armed Services of a nation and among the explorers who go to distant places and perhaps are in quest of distant wealth you'll find the prime professionals of peril. When they parade, the Pageant of Life has its maximum violence and suspense—in war and adventure. Human interest assumes a form more tense mid perils of the tropics, the bleak north or the height of the skies.

THE MARINES WERE SAYING "GOOD-BYE" TO HAITI. AFTER a visit by President Roosevelt to the island nation of the West Indies, the soldiers of the sea were ordered to bring finally to an end their eventful stay in the Black Republic. All over, boys—time for memories.

[194]

Uncle Sam's Leathernecks went into Haiti back in nineteen fifteen when things down there were in an intolerable snarl of bankruptcy and incessant revolutions. And did those gentlemen with necks of leather have trouble! Did they run into scrapping and tough going down there in that tropical land of mountains and jungle and black bushwhacking fighters! You can figure out the answer from the Congressional Medals that were handed out to the Marines in Haiti. Take this angle—the number of men who have won two Congressional Medals. There are four of them, and of the doubly decorated four two won America's highest military honor in Haiti. General Smedley D. Butler got one of his down there, and so did Dan Daly, the fightin'est Irishman of them all.

Dan served under Smedley Butler, chasing the Cacos, the black insurgents. Even then he was no spring chicken, but an old-timer with twenty-five years of service in the Marines. He had won his first Congressional Medal way back in the Boxer Rebellion. His hair was gray, his skin like leather —especially his neck. And was he hard-boiled!

A little detachment of Marines commanded by Smedley Butler was making a fighting jaunt through the wild country—and got lost. The Cacos sprang an ambush. It was at night. The Marines were fording a swift mountain stream when they were attacked. There was a wild scene of shooting and fighting in the darkness. They battled their way through. Several of their horses were killed—horses carrying guns and ammunition.

The Cacos were still after them. The Marines knew they

[195]

were in for another scrap. Smedley Butler called Sergeant Dan Daly.

"Better set up the machine gun, Sergeant."

"It was lost in the river, Sir."

That was a tough break. The machine gun was on one of the horses that had been killed while fording the river a mile back.

"Too bad," remarked Butler. "I guess we'll have to do without it."

Daly said nothing, and in the darkness he wasn't seen any more—not for some time. The Marines lay waiting for the attack, while the Cacos kept up a wild random fire from the surrounding jungle.

At length Dan Daly reappeared. He announced in a hard, matter-of-fact voice: "I've set up the machine gun, Sir!"

That was the first they knew of one of the bravest deeds in any war. On his own initiative, without any suggestion from his commanding officer, Dan Daly had fought his way through the swarm of Cacos back to the river. There, with the black insurrectos shooting at him, he swam back and forth until he found the dead horse with the machine gun. He strapped the gun on his own back, and fought his way along the return trail to his outfit.

He had scarcely returned when the Cacos made their rushing attack. The machine gun sprayed them with a deadly hail, and that decided the fight. No wonder Dan got his second Congressional Medal of Honor.

THE ARMY AIR CORPS NAMED ITS OUTSTANDING HERO OF nineteen thirty-nine, the flier to receive the Cheney award. He was First Lieutenant Harold Neely.

Piloting a big bomber, flying over Kansas, he ran into a dust storm. The air was so thick he couldn't see more than a few feet ahead. He was in an opaque, sightless murk of dust, flying blind. And just then his motor went dead. No motor—in the dust!

He had three Army men in the plane with him, and signaled them to jump, the parachute way. He himself prepared to bail out. Looking down through the dimness of the haze, he saw one parachute open, and then the other—but not the third. Only two of his three passengers had bailed out—so reflected First Lieutenant Harold Neely. The other, he figured, must still be in the back of the ship. So if he—the Lieutenant himself—bailed out, and left the ship to crash, that other passenger, the third Army man, would probably be killed in the smashup.

That was not Harold Neely's way. So he stuck to his bomber, as it went gliding and descending through the blinding dusk. Risking his life to save a life. He took the gamble of a sightless landing on ground he could not see. Down to earth he came in his disabled war plane. Controlling it as best he could, he maneuvered for as safe a contact with the ground as he could make. In the thick haze of dust, he managed to skid his plane along a field.

Down safe, First Lieutenant Neely was a bit irked, as he went to take a look at his passenger. Why hadn't the fellow jumped? He opened the back of the bomber—it was empty,

[197]

nobody there. What had happened was simple and tragic. The third passenger had indeed jumped. The Lieutenant had failed to see his parachute open—because it never did open. Parachute failure—and the passenger had been killed. Lieutenant Neely had risked his life to save a life that had already been lost. Whereupon the Air Corps proclaimed him its Number One Hero for nineteen thirty-nine.

AT BROCKTON, MASSACHUSETTS, THE JUDGE PASSED SENtence on Private Patuski—gave him six months in jail. That was a good deal of punishment for a soldier on furlough. But then consider the exploit that Private Patuski performed.

He was an artilleryman—and also a boxer. At camp Hulen, Texas, he was heavyweight champion of Battery H, Two Hundred and Eleventh Regiment of the Coast Artillery. A powerful soldier was Private Patuski—brawny arms and mighty fists. He was also a military policeman, which should have vouched for his excellent conduct—perfect behavior at all times. But Private Patuski also fancied himself as an amateur locomotive driver; and he set out to emulate the exploits of the legendary Casey Jones.

On leave from Camp Hulen, he went up to his native Massachusetts, and was on a passenger train speeding toward Brockton—when the inspiration seized him. He admitted he had had a few drinks and was in something of a haze. However, there was nothing hazy about what happened. Private Patuski climbed out onto the coal tender and then into the cabin of the locomotive. He pushed aside the engineer, nudged the fireman out of the way, and seized the throttle. Having a joy ride in a locomotive pulling ten cars loaded with passengers!

The engineer and fireman tried to get him out of there, away from the throttle—but it was no go. Private Patuski, the Army heavyweight boxer, was not easy to drive away from a throttle or anything else. The train was roaring its way into the Brockton station. Throttle wide open—what a ride!

The engineer and fireman summoned help—the conductor and the baggageman. All four hurled themselves on the amateur Casey Jones. The passenger train roared right on through the Brockton station before the engineer, fireman, conductor and baggageman were finally able to subdue Private Patuski. The engineer applied the airbrakes, and the train came to a sudden shrieking halt three hundred yards beyond the station.

So that was why the judge gave Private Patuski six months in jail. His Honor, however, said that he'd suspend the sentence if the Commandant at Camp Hulen, Texas, made the request.

The news didn't say how the Commandant felt about that. Maybe he replied: "Keep him, and give him the six months." Or maybe he growled, "Send him back to us."

Private Patuski was deeply concerned. He said he was just about to be promoted to the rank of Sergeant.

IN THE STATE OF WASHINGTON TWO SOLDIERS WERE CITED for special honors. They were heroes, and were cheered, but mingled with the cheers were a few loud laughs.

In the Western Army war games Private Glenn Sollie and Private Andrew Bearshield of the Fifteenth Infantry had been ordered to make their way to a bridge, and guard it. They were told to stand on duty at the bridge until they were relieved.

Private Glenn Sollie and Private Bearshield were faithful soldiers. They went and they guarded—and guarded. They stuck to it for three days and three nights—without food and without blankets. Then they were—no, not relieved, they were found. They were guarding the wrong bridge. The two brave warriors had lost their way and taken their battle stations at a bridge seven miles away from the one they were to guard. They might still be there, if the Fifteenth Infantry had not sent out a detail to look for them.

I suppose the two heroes might have been sent to the guardhouse for going to the wrong bridge, but they also deserved military honors for guarding it so long. They got the honors—plus a laugh or two.

AT HONOLULU, A MIDDLE-AGED MAN WAS IN A CLOTHING store buying a pair of trousers. He wanted something like the suit he was wearing—a tweed. The clerk was showing him one pair of pants and then another, when two sailors entered—petty officers. "Let's have a look at some socks and ties," called one of them, and the other sailor said the socks and ties had better be snappy. The clerk turned to the customer trying to buy a pair of trousers, and asked him to wait. "The Navy comes first, you know," the clerk explained with cheery emphasis.

The customer for trousers smiled wanly, stepped back, and waited. He was Admiral Kimmel, Commander-in-Chief of the American fleet.

A PARTY OF DANES, HEADED BY THE SECRETARY OF THE Danish Royal Geographical Society, went exploring in the glacial wilderness of the northern extremity of Iceland. A series of tremendous blizzards swept that glacial wild. Nothing was heard from the party. So a rescue expedition was sent out. Did they find the hapless adventurers frozen to death, victims of the ice? Not at all. The lost explorers were as warm as toast—snuggling in the hot crater of a live volcano. The crater was erupting steam to a height of three hundred and fifty feet—a giant stove up there in the frigid

Arctic. The missing scientists were warming their hands at the fires of Vulcan.

IN A SAN FRANCISCO COURT WAS ENACTED A CULMINATING incident in a bitter, fantastic tragedy. A petition had been filed to prevent the disclosure of the contents of the log of a ship. Keep that nautical record secret—otherwise a woman may go mad. The ship in question was the schooner *Wing On,* which had sailed to the South Seas on an adventure of romance. Pearl hunting, a quest for the shimmering, glowing gem of the sea. The pearl hunters were two married couples, Mr. and Mrs. Chester Thompson and Mr. and Mrs. Delton Conly. Out into the Pacific and down to the southern latitudes they navigated in their sailing ship, steering a course for lonely isles where brown men and black men dive for pearls. There a frightful misadventure befell them.

In the Fiji Islands some missionaries found the schooner *Wing On* wrecked, lodged on a coral reef. The pearl hunters had perished of hunger and thirst, all save one—Mrs. Chester Thompson. She remained hardly alive. They nursed her back to strength of body, but not of mind. She remained in a daze, a blank—her mental faculties shocked to numbness by the frightful ordeal. They brought her back home to California. There they were trying to restore her to normal.

The doctors attending her were afraid of one thing—

the log of the *Wing On*, the ship's record. The log had been written day after day by Mrs. Thompson's husband and the others, and its entries told the tale to the bitter end. The doctors were afraid it would be published and come to the attention of the dazed woman. Her memory was a blank, a merciful blank. Recollection must be brought to her gradually and skillfully by competent psychiatrists, otherwise she might forever lose her sanity. Hence the injunction proceedings in San Francisco—asking the court to prevent the publication of the log of the schooner *Wing On*.

AIRPLANES TOOK OFF FROM POINTS ON THE PACIFIC COAST, and headed northward. They were loaded to the limit with foodstuffs for the wild coast of Bering Sea, headed for Nome. That city so renowned for adventure in gold-rush days was in a desperate state. It was one blackened stretch. The people, burned out of house and home by a disastrous fire, were in straits for food and shelter.

In every state of the Union there was an individual here and there who might sink into an interval of thought, remembering the time when he was on the gold beach at Nome. I was one of them, one of the few thousand people who sometime or other had made the trip to Alaska and stopped a while among the sourdoughs left over from the big days of placer mining.

Back in the last century a surveyor was charting the then almost unexplored territory of Alaska. He came to an unknown place along the coast, and on the map he was making he wrote the word "name" and put a question mark after it, meaning that the place needed a name. Later on the authorities in studying his map misread his handwriting and thought the word "name" was—Nome. That's how the famous mining town came to be called Nome, synonym for gold.

The Nome gold rush began in 1898, when a miner or two stumbled upon nuggets and golden sand, and one of the most remarkable stampedes in history was on. A village of miserable shacks grew as if by magic into a modern town. In those mad, bad days Nome had a population as high as twenty thousand—the prospector, the adventuring tenderfoot, the sourdough, the gambler, the dance-hall girl, and the Eskimo—all the inimitable characters of a wild mining town in Alaska.

Long years later you'd still hear stories of Mother Woods, the hardest-boiled old gal that ever made hard-boiled men seem like timid doves. She came to Nome in her middle age, after having tramped the trail of every gold stampede in the North. She wore a sunbonnet, native Eskimo "mukluks" of sealskin for boots, and knee-length skirts which shocked everybody in that land of dance-hall girls. Her language made the most hardened sourdough gape with scandalized admiration. So they all called her "Mother."

Each year during the brief Arctic summer she fought

and swore and rampaged along the gold trail. Then at Nome she passed the winter taking care of the sick, the injured, the frozen—the most tender of nurses. Mother, indeed. When finally she got her mining claims snarled in a lawsuit and hadn't the money to keep her case in the courts, the whole town of Nome took up a collection and paid her legal expenses.

Then there was Joe Ripley, who had an Eskimo wife. Eskimo women are seldom beautiful, and Joe Ripley's wife was the ugliest of them all. He was a skinny runt. She, huge and fat. She used to beat him when he was drunk, which was most of the time.

Yet Joe was convinced, was always bragging to everyone—that his Eskimo wife was the most beautiful woman in the world. When he had a few drinks he would fight with fist, knife or pistol anyone who would exhibit the slightest doubt about his wife's dazzling beauty. Then he'd go to his shack, to the great fat scarecrow of an Eskimo, and she'd give him a couple of black eyes.

Then came the time when the fabulous gold city of Nome lay a mass of charred embers. Some said a spark on the roof of a hotel started the fire. Anyway, the flames swept uncontrollably in the cold Arctic breeze. Everyone in town fought the fire, men, women and children. They dynamited block after block, but couldn't halt the blaze. Only two buildings were left, one the headquarters of the Lomen Brothers, the Arctic reindeer magnates. The damages were said to be two million dollars, and everybody homeless. The

[205]

icebound Arctic winter was closing in. The season for ship traffic was over up there on the Polar Circle. The last ship had gone. So planes flew northward to the rescue.

FOR MANY A YEAR IN THE BLEAK NORTHERN SPACES OF THE Klondike, they discussed the mystery of Sir Arthur Curtis. What ever happened to that distinguished Englishman who vanished in the gold rush and was never seen again? What sort of foul play brought him to his end? Then, forty years later, in the rude cabins of the Northland, old-time miners fell to discussing that mystery more warmly than ever. For now a strange story had come to light, telling of the killing of Sir Arthur Curtis.

This account centered around a Captain H. P. Hilton. He had been one of the companions of the missing man on the gold-hunting expedition. Years later, in nineteen eight, Captain Hilton was serving with a British regiment in Canada. He had as his man a sergeant—James Martin. One day the captain showed the sergeant a newspaper clipping which stated that the missing Sir Arthur Curtis had been found, living a hermit's life in the Northland.

"I can't believe it," exclaimed the captain. "I killed Sir Arthur Curtis."

He went on to confide to the sergeant that back there in the Klondike the expedition consisting of a party of men had struck gold, and were coming out through the wild country with their hoard of nuggets packed on muleback. Their food supplies were stolen by roaming Indians, and the party was left in a dangerous plight. That night, Captain Hilton happened to awaken and saw someone driving their mules away. He followed, and saw it was Sir Arthur Curtis deserting his comrades, taking with him what little food was left, the mules, and the hoard of gold.

"I followed him, caught him, shot him, and buried him under a tree," the captain told his sergeant. He added that he took the food, mules and gold back to camp and said nothing.

Such was the story the captain told, and he pledged the sergeant to secrecy. "Never tell it until after I'm dead," he enjoined.

Two years later Captain Hilton was transferred to Hong Kong. The sergeant remained in Canada. In nineteen fifteen the captain was killed in action in France, in the fighting at Armentières, the town of Madamoiselle. The sergeant knew nothing of his death until nineteen twenty-six. Then when he heard it he thought, "What's the use of telling the story?"

Finally, however, a book was published in Canada, a book by Captain Roger Pocock, who had led the gold-hunting expedition of which Sir Arthur Curtis and Captain Hilton had been members.

He told the story so far as he knew it—and gave hints and surmises about the mystery of Sir Arthur Curtis. In answer to this the sergeant came forward and related his story. This aroused swift controversy. Some old-timers said the killing of Sir Arthur Curtis could not have happened that way—and the sourdoughs argued it out in the Northland.

COLONEL RICHARD C. SHAW HELD ONE OF THE MOST DANgerous jobs known to journalism. He was editor of that famous paper, *The Epitaph*, of Tombstone, Arizona. In nearly all books on the old-time wild and woolly two-gun West, you will find the Tombstone *Epitaph* prominently mentioned. Colonel Shaw used to say that the only tools he used were a paste pot, a pair of scissors, and a six-shooter. The paper was called *The Epitaph* because almost all the news in it consisted of obituary stories about the bad men of the Southwest. Those two-gun heroes used to die like the leaves in Vallombrosa.

Colonel Shaw was one of the friends of that picturesque old-time character, Wild Bill Hickok. One of his favorite stories concerned Wild Bill. Hickok and the colonel were standing up to the bar in Tombstone one evening. At the back of the bar was a huge mid-Victorian mirror surmounted with gilt cupids. Just as Wild Bill was raising a glass to his mouth he saw a face in that mirror. It was the face of a man who had sworn to kill Wild Bill on sight. The newcomer had his gun in his hand.

What did Wild Bill do? If he had turned around he would

have been killed instantly. Instead of that, he took swift aim in that cupid-framed mirror, shooting over his shoulder, plugged his enemy twice between the eyes, and without turning a hair, finished his drink.

Colonel Shaw was also fond of quoting one of the stories from his Tombstone *Epitaph*. It concerned another famous character, Wyatt Earp. The boys had elected Earp sheriff of Cochise County. When he was installed in office he made one simple statement: "Gentlemen," he said quietly, "I aim to keep the peace in Tombstone, if I have to shoot every doggone man in the place."

Finally Colonel Shaw went to join the two-gun men about whom he used to write. He was eighty years old. The irony was that after living through all those dangerous days, after seeing innumerable gun-fighters die with their boots on, he himself passed away in New York, run over by a taxi-cab.

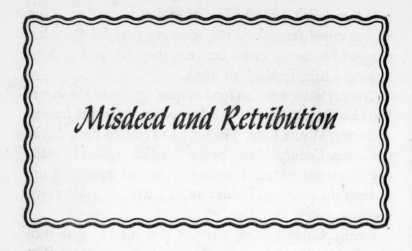

Misdeed and Retribution

THE darkest aspect of the Pageant of Life is crime and the penalties which it brings. Evil warpings of the human soul, the deed of blood, the profession of theft and violence, and the doom that society decrees for these. Yet the picture of misdeed and retribution is richly varied. In the prison is the death house, but in the prison, too, there's many a laugh. From agony to howling hilarity is the scope of that realm of human nature which has to do with the violation and enforcement of law.

A FIFTY-FOUR-YEAR-OLD BOOKKEEPER DREAMED A DREAM— and it was a bad dream. At Gary, Indiana, Ferdinand Dawm day after day sat over his ledgers and pushed his pen, living a gray, quiet life. But curious visions were fermenting in his brain. He dreamed of himself as a master-mind of crime, as one of those nefarious evil geniuses who plan and direct the operations of armies of crooks.

Then this middle-aged clerk started in to turn his evil dreams into realities. He got hold of two young men and persuaded them to become his followers. He outlined grandiose schemes of crime. He explained his plan to flood the brokers' offices of the country with forged stock certificates. He had a grand idea of a giant counterfeiting ring. Kidnaping, too, was a part of his criminal vision. He wanted to establish a whole chain of kidnaping gangs. In his unbridled fantasy he went even so far as to think up a gigantic plot for demoralizing the stock market and causing another panic.

The middle-aged bookkeeper sent one of his young disciples to consult a Chicago engraver on the subject of getting dies for making counterfeit money. He bade his other disciple to go to a prominent packing magnate and demand four thousand dollars by way of extortion. He primed both of his followers for a plan to kidnap another rich packer.

The would-be master mind really wasn't meant for crime at all. He was simple and guileless. One of his disciples was a more cunning fox than he. The young man went to the packer who was to be kidnaped and offered to expose the plot—in return for some money. They were all much too smart. The packer moved fast, and all three landed in jail.

The police found an arsenal of weapons in the possession of the middle-aged bookkeeper. They asked him what he wanted with all the firearms, and he replied simply that he thought some day he might take up a life of crime. In the end his wicked vision turned into the sordid reality of a dreary, cheerless cell in a jail.

IN LOS ANGELES THERE WERE TWO CLOSE FRIENDS, JOHN Peterson and Floyd Withrow. They were in the drug business, and Withrow in particular had done well for himself. He owned a highly prosperous concern, manufacturing drugs. Peterson, who was ten years younger than his friend, forgot that part of the Ten Commandments which talks about coveting your neighbor's property. He coveted that drug manufacturing business, and thought that the only way to get it was to bring about the death of his best friend. Not having the nerve to do it himself, he hired somebody else to do the killing. But the plot went wrong. Peterson was arrested, confessed, and did away with himself.

Then the bitterest part of that whole story came to light. The prosperous Withrow had actually made all preparations for giving his friend Peterson the drug business as a Christmas present. "I was going to tell him about it Christmas Day, the same time I gave our kids the bicycles I bought for them," said he. "As a matter of fact," he added, "I've been planning to hand it to him for a long time."

HERE'S A SITUATION FOR AN INGENIOUS MYSTERY STORY: A man was accused of a murder he did not commit. He was there when the crime was committed, but another man did it. He saw him do it with his own eyes. But this other man was innocent of the murder. It sounds complicated, but life arranged the plot—life in the big city.

Dominick Zerbonio came to New York, an immigrant from Italy. He worked hard, saved his money, and presently was the thriving owner of a small trucking business. One day two gangsters came to him and tried to shake him down, the old blackhand racket. He refused. They suggested he ought to come and talk it over with the big boss of the gang. Dominick said "All right," and went.

In a stuffy East Side flat he met the big boss. An argument started—between the big boss and one of his henchmen. Suddenly the henchman pulled a gun and shot the boss, who crumpled to the floor with bloodstains on his face and chest.

Then swiftly the door was burst open. Two detectives, flashing badges, appeared. They grabbed Dominick. The other blackhanders nodded. Yes, they said, Dominick had done the shooting. A doctor in a white coat appeared, examined the big boss, and pronounced him dead. And the charge against Dominick was murder!

He protested that he was innocent. They laughed. They started to take him to jail. Someone suggested the thing could be fixed. Dominick, scared to death, jumped at the chance. After much palaver, the policemen said they would let him go and forget about him for three thousand dollars.

He paid two thousand. He had to mortgage his store and trucks to do it. They demanded the balance. He could not get it. In despair Dominick went to police headquarters and told his story. And that's when the police raided one of the boldest and most ingenious extortion gangs in the history of New York.

The killing of the big boss had been faked from one end to the other. The pistol fired at him had been loaded with blanks. The blood on his face and chest had come out of a bottle of ketchup. The supposed detectives and supposed doctor, too, had been members of the gang, playing their parts. They had been working the game far and wide, fake murders, fake abductions of women, fake everything. But the prison sentences they got were no fake.

THE CANVAS THAT WAS LIFTED WAS A WATTEAU WORTH a hundred thousand dollars. The police of all Europe looked for that precious bit of paint-upon-canvas. All the time it was only a hundred yards from the museum—in the apartment of a young artist named Serge Boguslavsky. After a couple of months he walked into the Palace of Justice carrying that painting under his arm, wrapped in crumpled paper.

It was the artistic temperament, he explained, that had led him to swipe it. For days he had been at work in the Louvre copying the Watteau. As he did so he became indignant. The painting had been renovated, retouched by order of the authorities of the Louvre, and young Boguslavsky thought it was a badly botched up job. Instead of repairing it, the retouchers had spoiled it. That's why he took it away, as a protest.

After he had made this explanation to a magistrate, the law called in art experts. They agreed with the young painter. They said the masterpiece had been painted over, badly retouched. Whereupon the law dealt mildly with him, and inflicted hardly more than nominal punishment. You know, Messieurs, the artistic temperament.

One amusing feature of the episode was that the young man said he hadn't the slightest difficulty in taking that hundred-thousand-dollar canvas out of the Louvre. He just waited until he was alone in front of it, unhooked it from the wall, put it under his coat, and walked out. His story inspired a reporter on a Parisian newspaper, who proceeded to do the same thing with another painting hanging in the Louvre. He carried it out in the folds of a newspaper, walked a few blocks away from the museum, then telephoned the curator and told him about it. All of which delighted the Parisians, who loved nothing more than a laugh at the expense of authority.

THE ASSASSINATION OF AN ARCHBISHOP. THE CRIME IN NEW York was interwoven with mysteries of political terror in a dim corner of Asia. The story was that the killers executed a sinister decree, the mandate of the Tashnag, a secret order to assassinate the archbishop. And that led to strange affairs in a strange distant land. It's always beguiling the way some outlandish thing can happen in some outlandish place and can reach around the globe, right into our own work-a-day midst, to cause fantastic events among us.

One of the oldest and most historical countries on earth is Armenia—and one of the most tragical. For an age we were told of the oppression the Christian Armenians suffered at the hands of the Moslem Turk. Then came the climax, the World War, the Armenian nation almost wiped out by the fanatic sons of Islam. We heard a great deal about that. But what happened to the Armenian nation after that? The question was brought into vivid light by the murder of the archbishop in New York.

Most of what was left of the Armenian nation was in Russia, in those wild mountains, the Caucasus. The Christian Armenians used to be under the dominion of the Mohammedan Turk. Now they were under the dominion of the anti-religious Red Communists. That made a situation loaded with social explosive. A large proportion of the Armenians were bitterly hostile to the Soviets, but there was one faction within the Armenian Church that was playing ball with the Red rulers of Moscow. The head of that pro-Bolshevik faction was Archbishop Leon Lourian.

They nominated him to come to the United States, to be the spiritual head of the Armenians over here. He made no secret of his Communist sympathies. When Litvinoff, the

Soviet Commissar of Foreign Affairs, came to the United States to negotiate with President Roosevelt for the recognition of Russia, a grand banquet was held in his honor in New York. Only one church dignitary was present—the Armenian Archbishop, Leon Lourian. In Chicago they celebrated "Armenian Day," and that same archbishop refused to make his speech until an anti-Soviet Armenian flag had been removed from the stands—which created a disturbance. There was another disturbance for similar reasons when the archbishop attended a big Armenian festivity in Massachusetts. Trouble and dangerous doings were brewing. They came about swiftly and in spectacular fashion.

Away in distant Armenia, in the craggy Caucasus Mountains, there was a mysterious terrorist society—the Tashnag. It was the central Armenian revolutionary organization waging secret warfare against the Red regime. It had its ramifications and tentacles all over the world, wherever Armenians were. And they said the Tashnag decreed the death of the archbishop.

So the day came when the bustling Western metropolis of New York was startled by an act of melodramatic terror. The archbishop, of towering stature, gray-bearded, majestic in full canonicals, with a golden miter on his head and his shepherd's staff in his hand, was stabbed to death by a party of swift-acting killers. He was struck down by knife thrusts, as he led the Sunday procession up the aisle of his church.

THE STATE POLICE, IN THE MOUNTAINS OF WESTERN PENN-sylvania, battled their way through snowdrifts to reach a remote farmhouse. They were bringing aid to an injured woman, a woman wounded by shotgun fire. They were also checking up on a fantastic tale of violence and killing, a story of how the wounded woman had been compelled by a man—to shoot him.

Farmer Ralph Caldwell employed a farm hand named Glenn Plants. Then for some reason or other, the farmer discharged the farm hand, who thereupon declared he'd get even. It turned into one of those hill-country feuds. At night the Caldwells, husband and wife, were in their kitchen. Suddenly at a kitchen window appeared the feud-ing farm hand. He had a shotgun, and was aiming it through the window. The wife sought to shield her husband, tried to throw herself in front of him, as the shotgun blasted. The husband fell to the floor, killed. The wife was wounded in the arms from the spray of shot.

Thereupon the killer forced his way into the house, where the most fantastic part of it all occurred. The killer forced a sixteen-year-old boy who worked on the farm, forced him to witness what happened. He bade the widow of the man he had just slain to shoot him—she with her wounded and bleeding arms. He put the muzzle of the shotgun against his own chest, holding the gun out, and told her to pull the trigger. She did, the gun roared, and the killer fell, the life blasted out of him.

Then the woman, suffering from her painful injuries, took her two small children, and with the boy farm worker they started out through the snowy night, bound for the nearest neighbor's house, seven miles away. They trudged and toiled through blizzard and deep snow. When they reached the neighbor's house, the neighbor got to the telephone and called the state troopers. These battled their way to the scene, bringing help and checking and verifying the mad tale.

NOW A STORY WITH A MORAL FOR NEWSPAPER MEN. A bandit walked into a hotel in Chicago and held up the clerk at the desk. The clerk recognized him as the same robber who had held him up two weeks before. The crook was angry. He was annoyed.

"Now, listen, big boy," he grumbled, "that other time I was here, I took fifty dollars from you. Remember, just fifty bucks. And the next day the newspapers said I got two hundred."

He was telling the honest truth. He had stolen fifty dollars on his previous burglarious visit to the hotel. The newspapers had got it wrong and said it was two hundred.

"Now, listen, feller, that wasn't right," the crook went on. "It got me into plenty of trouble. When I went home I told my wife the honest truth and said I got fifty dollars, and the next day she read in the newspaper that I got two hundred, and there ain't nothing I can say that will make her believe any different. She thinks I lost the rest of the money in a crap game, and she's been bawling me out ever since.

"And so I'm telling you, I want you to be sure the newspaper reporters get the story right this time, because my wife will be reading the papers and I don't want her to think I'm holding out on her."

The hotel clerk had just fifteen dollars in the till. The bandit took it and departed with the final injunction: "Remember, this is only fifteen bucks, and don't you have the reporters saying twenty-five or a hundred and fifty."

Yes, a salutary lesson. We must be careful to get the news straight or we'll be getting robbers and bandits in trouble with their wives.

AT PARK RAPIDS, MINNESOTA, A TRAMP WALKED INTO A restaurant and asked the proprietor for a free meal. The hobo looked so hungry and bedraggled that the sympathetic restaurant man said, "O.K., what'll yuh have, ham or a stack of wheats?" The tramp sat down at a table and had a good meal, a first-class handout.

As the hobo was leaving, he walked up to the proprietor and even bummed a cigarette. He fished in a pocket for a match, and along with the match he carelessly pulled out a twenty-dollar bill.

"Say, what's that," shouted the proprietor. "You come

in here bumming a meal, and you've got twenty bucks."
And he grabbed the banknote.

"But this was supposed to be a free meal," the hobo protested.

"Not on your life," responded the restaurant man. "I'll just take thirty-five cents out of this twenty."

"Just remember, buddy," said the tramp. "I don't want you to do this—I'm not asking you."

"Is zat so," responded the restaurant man, and he handed the hobo nineteen dollars and sixty-five cents in change.

The unhappy ending of the story is that when the proprietor took the money to the bank he found that the twenty-dollar bill he had taken from the hobo was counterfeit.

IN PROVIDENCE, RHODE ISLAND, A MAN WAS WAITING IN line to buy a ticket to the theater. Two men jostled him, and a minute later he discovered that his pocketbook with all his money was gone. He chased after the two, caught up with one, and yelled: "Give me back my pocketbook, give me back my money!"

"I haven't got it," the man replied.

The victim continued to roar, and a crowd was gathering. Whereupon the man charged with theft demanded: "How much was in your pocketbook?"

"Twenty-five dollars," howled the victim.

The accused whipped some bills out of his pocket, and handed twenty-five dollars to the victim, who let him go.

Later he told the police that the actual amount in the stolen pocketbook had really been fourteen dollars, not twenty-five. So he nearly doubled his money on the transaction.

MANY A STORY HAS A BEAUTIFUL BEGINNING LIKE THIS NEXT one. But all too often the end is just hardhearted. Now wouldn't you call it a beautiful beginning when a police sergeant, who had been a choir boy, hears the refrain of an old well-remembered hymn? Sergeant Harry Schuler of the Chicago police was in a restaurant when he heard a dishwasher in the kitchen singing with full-throated fervor, that fine old hymn: "Shall We Gather at the River, the Beautiful, Beautiful River?"

There was a world of sentiment in the sounds as the dishwasher caroled the refrain of that "beautiful river." The police sergeant, who had been a choir boy, knew his hymnbook, and was familiar with the way a minister leads the singing. That dishwasher must have been a pastor at one time, he reflected.

Here's where the hardhearted part comes in. The sergeant took a careful look at a police circular he carried—list of men wanted. Then he went out into the kitchen and arrested Carl Anderson, formerly a clergyman of Washington, who was wanted on a charge of deserting his wife and child. A hardhearted ending, indeed. But let's be idealistic and hope it resolved into a beautiful ending. Let's suppose that as a result of the hymn singing in the kitchen the former minister was reunited with his wife and child and that they were happy for ever and ever.

AN EXTRAORDINARY SIGHT WAS WITNESSED AT KANSAS CITY. A truck heaped high with rubbish speeding along, and on top of the stack of rubbish—a woman. Yelling wildly, waving her hands. Some might have thought that the lady was just being carted off to the junk heap with the rubbish, but it was worse than that.

She was a housewife, who had hired two men with a truck to remove the trash from the basement of her home. They removed it all right—and not only that. Along with the trash they loaded up a big sack of walnuts, little Johnny's new sled which he got for Christmas, a gas water heater, and all the family laundry. The indignant lady climbed aboard the truck to retrieve these belongings, and just then the truck started off, the men driving away. So there was the lady on top of the high heap of rubbish, protesting and gesticulating, as the truck hit it up along the highway. It hit all the rough spots too—for the rogues in the driver's seat were trying to shake her off, trying to bounce her from her precarious perch.

She got the bushel of walnuts and tossed it into the road, also Johnny's new sled. But just then the truck hit a particularly big bump, and the lady went bouncing off into the roadway. There she picked herself up and retrieved the walnuts and the sled. She lost the water heater and the family laundry, but she retained the two dollars she had promised to pay the two men for carting away the rubbish.

"THIS IS WHAT I CALLS A BLOOMIN' SHIME." IMAGINE A London Bobbie saying that in his most indignant cockney. A mean trick was played on the English police, and a woman did it. She was a well-known fraud. Sixteen times she had been sent to jail for larceny. Released after her latest prison sentence, she came out of jail without twopence, and wanted to get to the north of England. That was a problem, but the lady proceeded to solve it.

She went to the police, said she was a Scotland Yard detective, and told them to get a car for her right away. She was after two men who had committed a crime. The local Bobbies were eager to oblige a female Sherlock Holmes from Scotland Yard, and they got the car. She was driven to Hersham, and there she made a bluff at searching a house; then she had the police drive her to London, where she en-

[224]

tered a prominent club. When she came out she told the Bobbies in the car that she had word that she must trail five Americans who had gone to Torquay. They took her to Torquay, several hundred miles away, and then on various pretexts she had them drive her from place to place. The police in the car paid for her meals and other expenses.

It was when they had taken her all the way to northern England that she made her big mistake. She tried to buy a fur coat on credit and used the police officers with her as evidence that her credit was good. The gullible Bobbies at last got a touch of inspiration. They communicated with Scotland Yard, and then it was indeed a "bloomin' shime," because the next thing on the program was the arrest of the clever lady. She went back to jail, but she certainly had had an extensive and pleasant tour of England. And didn't she twist those bally British police around her little finger? Well, rawther!

THIS IS THE STORY OF A PERFECT LADY, QUIET, WELL BRED, charming manners. A perfect lady, except in one small detail—robbery. A model of the social graces, she made only one slip, only one faux pas—she held people up with a gun. They called her the "Woman in Black." She dressed simply and with excellent taste, preferring that color of aristocratic reserve—black. They also called her the "Girl with the Handbag," because of the stick-up technique she used—so deft and so ladylike.

She made the headlines with one robbery that was a monument of boldness—only, it's hardly proper to apply the word "bold" to such a perfect lady. After having held up a Chinese restaurant and got away with the contents of the cash drawer, and after having committed several other banditries, the perfect lady and her elegant handbag achieved the height—of nerve. But then a perfect lady wouldn't be nervy. So let's just say—the height of something.

A policeman in full uniform, blue coat, long night stick, and a pistol and holster, was sitting not more than twenty feet away from the cashier's desk in a restaurant on upper Broadway, when in stepped the perfect lady. Seeing the big and burly cop, the expression of her eye never changed from that sedate aloofness which mothers teach their daughters. She stepped to the cashier's desk—the proximity of the policeman didn't bother her at all. Why should it, with that exquisite handbag technique of hers?

The cashier saw a good-looking young woman in her early twenties, with finely chiseled features, black eyes, fashionably dressed in black. She asked for a couple of packs of cigarettes, and the cashier noticed that her voice was well modulated, with educated accent. Then he noticed something else—something astonishing.

The perfect lady raised her handbag and opened it so that the cashier could look into it. He saw—a pistol, the lady's well-manicured hand grasping the gun, a slender finger on the trigger. And she never took it out of the bag.

"Hand over the money," said she politely.

He did—all the cash he had in the cash drawer. She deftly stowed it away in her handbag beside the gun.

The policeman twenty feet away saw nothing. Who would suspect a lady's handbag? Who would dream of walking over and peering into that feminine carry-all, in which womanhood may have almost anything stowed? So the robbery was carried out under the nose of the law.

The getaway was quiet and dignified, as the girl with the handbag tripped prettily out into the street and took a taxi. Then the cashier let out a roar—"Robbers! Police! Robbers!" The astounded cop at the near-by table got the story as quickly as he could, dashed out, took another taxi in pursuit—vain pursuit. She was gone.

Half an hour later the taxi she had taken returned to its stand in front of the restaurant. The driver said the girl with the handbag had merely stepped into his cab and told him with quiet dignity that she was in a hurry to get to Seventy-first street. He took her there, never suspecting that she was aught but a perfect lady.

ON THE ROOF OF A FASHIONABLE NEW YORK APARTMENT house, where there were benches and shrubs, a good-looking blonde sat sewing. It's always an agreeable sight, a smartly-dressed, attractive young woman working away at the ancient feminine handicraft of stitching and mending. A detective came wandering onto the roof. He was looking for a burglar, trying to solve the mystery of a series of robberies in the swanky apartment house. He looked at the cute blonde, as she sat there busily sewing. He noted that she was stitching her handkerchief, which was all right. But he also observed that she was sewing with a key, not a needle, a door key. And that was an astonishing thing to behold.

The detective walked over to the blonde and remarked, "Well, this is the first time in my life I ever saw a girl use a key for sewing."

And the blonde answered, "So what?"

This was what: The burglaries had been committed with a pass key that gave admittance to all the apartments in the building. The pass key had been swiped from the place where it hung in the lobby of the apartment house. The key with which the blonde was nonchalantly sewing—was the pass key. Presently the blonde was confessing to the robberies.

DOWN IN TEXAS POLICE TOOK INTO CUSTODY AN EARNEST and erudite student, a tall striking brunette who proudly proclaimed that she held the degree of G.S.L. That signified—Graduate of Shoplifting. She said she did her studying in the Oklahoma Penitentiary, where she spent some time among accomplished shoplifters who acted as professors. Having been released with the degree of G.S.L., she teamed up with another earnest scholar, Marie Barrow by name. Sister of the late and notorious Texas bandit, Clyde Barrow, who ended his career in a blaze of gunfire.

The two shoplifting ladies sojourned in the town of Wills Point, and the police say they just about lifted the town. They shoplifted the whole place. For days the Wills Point merchants noticed how their stocks of merchandise were dwindling at an astonishing rate, but there was no corresponding increase in the cash register. It looked as if the merchandise stocks were evaporating.

The two lady lifters were finally caught, their automobile found to be crammed with drygoods and groceries.

The graduate of shoplifting boasted of her degree of G.S.L.: "In my course at the Oklahoma Penitentiary," she said, "I learned how to conceal even canned goods under my clothing. Why, I can do a tap dance," she bragged, "and the canned goods won't fall out."

This apt scholar was soon on her way back for postgraduate work in the penitentiary. They figured that when she got out again she'd probably be able to lift the Empire State Building.

A CURIOUS COMEDY TOOK PLACE IN A BRANCH OF A BIG New York bank. There appeared before one of the tellers' windows a wavering old man with long white whiskers who produced a bank deposit book and a letter. The letter was signed with the name of the owner of the passbook asking the teller to give the bearer of the letter three hundred dollars and charge it to that account.

The teller took another look at the old gentleman who produced the passbook. Something about those long white whiskers didn't seem natural. He called the police, and two detectives arrived. One of them said: "Them whiskers don't look real to me." So he gave the whiskers a yank. The old gentleman said "Ow!" Not because his whiskers had been pulled out, but because they snapped back on a rubber band.

The old gentleman turned out to be no gentleman. He— rather she—was a woman. When she was brought into the police court she denied that she had made an attempt at grand larceny.

"How do you make that out?" said the magistrate.

"It is my own money," said the woman.

Whereupon she proceeded to prove it. She explained that she had gone through the masquerade in order to gather experience. She was a trained nurse by profession, but decided she would like to write books. Before writing the books she wanted to get some local color.

"Well, have you had enough?" asked the magistrate.

"Enough and plenty," said the lady. "I am satisfied."

IN THE ANCIENT LEGEND, TANTALUS OFFENDED THE GODS. His punishment was eternal thirst—and he was tantalized. He stood in water up to his chin, but when he tried to drink it the water receded. Luscious fruits hung before him and tantalized him, but when he reached for them they moved away and eluded his grasp. That was as stupendous a punishment as the mind of classical antiquity could imagine. But the authorities in the Eastern Penitentiary in Philadelphia were able to imagine something even more drastic, in a way—a modern version of the legend of Tantalus.

One day there was a riot in the prison—a riot against the prison food. It was started by ten ringleaders who vowed they'd never eat another bit of penitentiary fare. The trouble was suppressed. The ten leaders were isolated in a punishment block. They kept their vow not to eat the prison food—a hunger strike. For five days they didn't touch a morsel. They gritted their teeth, and kept on starving.

The prison authorities were in a quandary. It would be awkward to have the ten men die of hunger. So they tried a stratagem—a stratagem consisting of great platters of sizzling sirloin steaks, baked potatoes, and smothering heaps of onions. These were taken into the cell block where the ten hunger strikers were keeping their fast. The aroma drifted through the cells—steak, potatoes, and onions—especially the savory perfume of fried onions. The nostrils of the hunger strikers were assailed. Their mouths watered. It was the story of Tantalus brought down to date. They stood it as long as they could, and then broke down—it was too tantalizing.

[231]

"We'll eat," they shouted. "Bring on the grub."

The grub was brought on—but that's the irony of it. In front of the ten convicts was placed the same old prison food—oatmeal, coffee, and bread. They ate it, subjugated by a stratagem that out-tantalized Tantalus.

THE BEST HORSE THIEF IN AMERICA WENT TO HIS ETERNAL reward. In the Philadelphia Eastern Penitentiary, Abe Buzzard of the horse-stealing Buzzards departed for the promised land. And if there were any horses in that promised land—look out! Abe was eighty-five. In the cell next to the one he occupied for so long, his brother Joe Buzzard, aged seventy-five, sat grieving and lamenting. "Abe was the best dern horse thief this country ever had." That was the way Joe Buzzard eulogized the dear departed. And in the Welsh mountain section of Pennsylvania folks were discussing the merits of the celebrated horse thief who spent fifty of his eighty-five years in prison.

He was the leader of a gang of three brothers, Abe, Joe, and Ike. They were called the Three Buzzards, and became a legend. History relates that when the Buzzard boys were children, their father was killed in the Civil War. Their mother remarried, upon which Abe, Joe and Ike took to the hilltops. There were a number of other children in the family, but they disappeared in the anonymous nothingness of respectability. The Three Buzzard boys lived as a gang of outlaws, stealing chickens, farm products, clothing—and especially horses. In their long career they were frequently arrested. How long they stayed arrested depended on the jail. If it was a good jail, with plenty to eat and pleasant surroundings, they served their sentences, and commonly got religion while doing so. If they didn't like the food and companionship, they escaped.

Some people might say they came to a bad end, but the Three Buzzards regarded it as a good end, a good jail. Abe was arrested the last time for stealing chickens, but he never was so good at chickens. His genius was horses. After that chicken Waterloo he made his permanent home in the Philadelphia Eastern Penitentiary. Two years later, Joe Buzzard strayed into New Jersey, where the state troopers got him for stealing something or other. His only defense was that they had plenty more on him in Pennsylvania than they had in New Jersey. So his plea was that they take him back to Pennsylvania so that he could join his brother Abe in the penitentiary. That was duly accomplished. The history I have consulted doesn't say what happened to Ike Buzzard. Maybe he got discouraged because he couldn't compete with Brother Abe in horse stealing.

AT SANTA FE, NEW MEXICO, A MAN APPEARED AT THE State Penitentiary and told the warden he was Ed Sweet and he'd like to look the prison over. That meant he had to dig up the usual visitor's fee of twenty-five cents. He paid it cheerfully. A guard showed him around, and he tipped the guard a quarter.

"Well, this certainly is a fine classy cooler," he said to the warden at the end of the tour. "I like this place. Yes, nice spot. I think I'll stay."

"What do you mean?" asked the warden. "How do you get that way?"

"Oh, it looks like a cheery comfortable lockup," replied Ed. "I think I'll just put up here for a while."

"Yeah? How come?" queried the warden.

"Here's how," replied Ed.

He pulled out of his pocket a paper which showed that he had been convicted of stealing automobile tires, and had a year in prison coming to him. He had been at large and very sensibly had looked over the jail before deciding whether or not to serve his sentence.

And all the warden could do was look blank and mumble: "Well, just make yourself at home, Ed, make yourself at home."

THREE BANDITS WENT TO THE CHAIR IN ILLINOIS, AND THE singular thing was the grim scene before the execution. The three were offered a chance to gamble to determine the order in which they would die. Flip a coin. Many a time they had enjoyed gambling. Many a time they flipped a coin in the hazard of chance, to see who'd win the money. But this time the gambling was too forbidding. They refused. Allowed to choose the order in which they would go, they couldn't bear the clink of the coin on the stone floor. They decided to walk to the chair in the sequence of their cells along death row at Joliet, the nearest man first, the farthest man last.

*
=

IN CHICAGO A JUDGE GAVE A MAN A SENTENCE, WHICH turned out to be altogether too severe, so the judge decided to serve the sentence himself. It happened this way:

Judge John Zbarbaro was dispensing justice when Thomas Delmato was brought, charged with disorderly conduct. The defendant had a set of books with him—five volumes of Victor Hugo. Where he got them was not revealed.

"I'll sentence you to jail," announced the judge, "and you'll have to stay there long enough to read those books."

So the defendant was taken to the hoosegow along with the five bulky volumes of Victor Hugo.

The next day the judge asked how much the prisoner had read in the course of twenty-four hours. He discovered that Delmato had succeeded in wading through just one page and a half of Hugo's prose. That made the judge stop and think. At that rate of speed it would take the prisoner three years to read the five volumes, which meant that the judge had sentenced the unfortunate to three years in prison on nothing more than a disorderly conduct charge.

The judge pondered over the mistake he had made, and arrived at a judgment worthy of Solomon. He called off the prisoner's sentence and had him released from jail. At the same time the judge took the sentence upon himself. He carried the books home with the announcement that he would read them.

FOUR YEARS OF TERROR, A PROLONGED TORMENT OF LINGER-ing dread—that was the story of what might have seemed to be a glittering stroke of luck. Nothing more common than for people to say, "Gee, if I could only find something —walking along, find a treasure!" Ethel Hinton found a treasure, but it was as though she had picked up an evil curse, a handful of ghostly misfortune.

She was a Negro woman employed sweeping out a fashionable dress shop. One day while she was plying her broom she swept up something white and gleaming. It was a hundred-thousand-dollar pearl necklace. It had been lost by Mrs. Grafton W. Minot, wife of a banker, who at one time had been secretary to the United States embassy in Berlin.

The Negro woman gaped in amazement as she handled the flowing strands, two strands, one with one hundred and ten perfectly graduated pearls, the other with a hun-dred and twenty-nine. The two strands were held together by a clasp set with twelve diamonds. Ethel Hinton put aside her broom. She hid the fabulous necklace. She wouldn't have to sweep out a store any longer. She went home and told her husband. They agreed to keep the treasure of pearls. They saw an advertisement from the woman who had lost the jewels, but decided to hold on to the fortune.

They were holding on to evil fortune. The possession of the pearl necklace haunted them with hidden fears. They were terrified at the thought of trying to dispose of it. Every day deepened their anxiety. Months went by, years—four years. The only thing they ventured was to detach some of the small diamonds from the clasp and pawn them.

The police said it was simply the nemesis of the pearl necklace that gave them away. James Hinton, the husband, lived so deep in brooding fear that the terror of the necklace set its mark on him. His movements became stealthy. He went slinking about, with a harassed look to right and left. So it was that two detectives saw him come out of a building, and his furtive air made them suspicious. They stopped him, searched him, and in one pocket found the necklace. Husband and wife were in difficulties. Yet they were relieved to be free—free of the gleaming curse, the ominous luster of the pearls.

IN A JAPANESE STREET WAS A SUDDEN COMMOTION. A MAN leaped at another one and started beating him with shrieking fury.

"Confess," he yelled.

"No," gasped his victim, "I didn't do it!"

This was the culminating scene of a Japanese tragedy —a man sent to prison for a crime he had not committed.

Long years in the past a traveler was robbed and killed on a lonely road, and Ishimatsu Yoshida was accused. Two witnesses against him sealed his fate. He went to prison, where he stayed for twenty-three years. Finally he was released, and immediately began a hunt for his two accusers. One of them he soon found, and forced that witness to admit his testimony had been false—and that the crime had actually been committed by the accusing witness. Thereupon Ishimatsu's search was intensified. Month after month he hunted far and wide—until after a year he found his man, spied him on the street, and flew at him with the bitterness of twenty-three years in prison.

"Confess that you committed the murder!" he yelled as he beat the man with mad fury.

The other denied it, until finally, under the terror of the attack, he admitted: "Yes, I confess, I killed him." Whereupon Ishimatsu Yoshida reopened his case and conviction, and procured a retrial and exoneration. But he couldn't get back those twenty-three years.

A British captain in Palestine found himself confronted with an exceedingly unmilitary problem. A Jewish watchman was found murdered in an Arab village. Of course, as our English friends say, "that sort of thing can't go on, don't you know—simply isn't done!" So the British captain was there to execute justice. But he couldn't find anybody to enforce it on. Apparently, there was no other place so full of completely innocent people as that Arab village.

It was the custom of the English, in administering law, to follow, so far as possible, the legal customs of the country. By the law of the Arabs, if a man was found murdered and his murderer could not be found, the community was held responsible. Arab law did not always demand an eye for an eye, or a tooth for a tooth. It also held that if a man were slain, the crime could be wiped out—expiated by the payment of a sufficient sum of money, a few pounds of gold.

Unfortunately, there was no money to speak of in that village. "All right," said the captain, "then you shall pay in grain." But there was so little grain about the place that it wasn't enough to pay for the life of the Jewish watchman.

The captain sighed and exclaimed: "Oh, that I had a Daniel with me, to tell me what to do in the judgment seat!" At that moment he espied a couple of camels browsing by the wayside. So he said to the elders of the village: "Lo, these beasts will make up what is lacking." Whereupon he proceeded to seize the camels.

At that a loud cry of lament arose. A wailing woman

threw herself at the feet of the British captain, pleading: "Have mercy, I am a widow and in all the world I have nothing save these two poor camels."

The captain turned to the elders of the village and said: "Does this woman speak truth?"

And the elders replied: "Protector of the poor, she speaks indeed the truth. Her husband is dead long since, and all she has in the world are her camels. For behold, no man will wed with her, for she hath a shrewish tongue."

At that the captain exclaimed: "Go, woman, take your camels and be gone."

He decided there was nothing he could do to enforce justice, and went his way. Then later—too late—it was learned that the camels were not the widow's, the place was full of hidden grain, and all the Arabs had concealed wealth. Allah had been merciful.

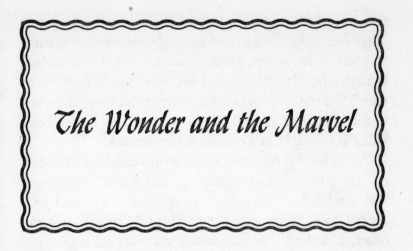

The Wonder and the Marvel

SOME of the things that happen and are recorded are of the wildest improbability—a tax on credulity. There's the thing of wonder—can it be? There's the occult happening, the apparent manifestation of the supernatural, the miracle. There's the coincidence that staggers all sense of probability and the utterly freak affairs for which there's no accounting. Mighty close to tall stories some of these factually reported events appear to be. So use your own judgment.

THEY HAD A HAUNTED SPEAKEASY IN ATLANTIC CITY. DUR-ing the prohibition era the place flourished with all the glitter and criminal doings of the period. Later, after repeal, it was turned into a legal place of festivity and high-jinks. Then one night at the tick of midnight, when the jazz band was blaring its loudest, a woman screamed and then sobbed hysterically, "It's Mervine. I see him there—John Mervine." She thought she saw the ghost of the swagger owner of the place back in speakeasy days, the man who had been killed at midnight in a quarrel over a woman.

On nights that followed, other people cried out that they saw the ghost—just at midnight. Then it was remembered that a subsequent owner of the speakeasy who had succeeded John Mervine had gone violently insane. Still another, a woman, had committed suicide—leaving an explanation that a curse had been placed on the building. The wife of the most recent owner had fallen down a stairway and broken three ribs, and his daughter had dropped unconscious on the way to school.

So the festive night club, formerly a haunt of gaiety, became known as a house of horror. Patrons heard all kinds of strange noises and other spectral manifestations. They said that the ghost of John Mervine passed along the tables of the merrymakers and knocked over glasses with an unseen hand—at midnight, always at midnight.

Business went bad, as the awestricken patrons ceased to come to the house of horror, and finally the haunted speakeasy was abandoned as a place of night-club revelry. They turned it into an athletic club, hoping that the ghost wouldn't bother the ping-pong, hand balls and dumbbells.

*
=

THE DRUGGISTS OF AMERICA, AT THE STATLER HOTEL IN Boston, presented a special gold medal to a Kentucky druggist—all because he dreamed a dream. No, he didn't dream that he ran a drug store entirely devoted to drugs. Frank Miller of Louisville, Kentucky, dreamed that he was going into his drug store in a rowboat.

He was so convinced of the reality of his dream that he told all his friends in Louisville, warned them to be ready, warned them that the Ohio River would soon be rising, urged his fellow Louisville druggists to make emergency preparations. He even made an appeal over the radio for funds to combat the flood that he had dreamed about.

He did all this just one week before the Ohio went on the rampage, the greatest flood in American history. Then Frank Miller, instead of sitting back and saying "I told you so," filled all flood-victim prescriptions free of charge at his place, and directed relief. Later the Druggists of America took a vote and decided that Frank Miller should be proclaimed "America's Gold Medal Druggist" for the year.

THE LONDON *DAILY MAIL* GATHERED A WHOLE FLOCK OF stories about dreams that came true. One was from an English farmer, who wrote that he had been afflicted with blindness for three years. One night he had a vivid dream in which he was reading the Bible to his wife. He awoke and remembered just what chapter of the Bible—the fourteenth chapter of St. John. He asked his wife to get the Bible and turn to the fourteenth chapter of John. Then he took the book and read the chapter just as he had done in the dream. His eyesight had returned. He had dreamed that he was no longer blind, and awoke to find it true.

SCIENTISTS AND MYSTICS ALIKE WERE VIVIDLY INTERESTED in the mysterious case of a Hungarian girl. She was fifteen years old. She was stricken with influenza and seemed to be dying. She seemed, in fact, to be dead—for a few moments. Then suddenly she revived and recovered quickly. It seemed as if she had come back to life—a different person. For she spoke, not Hungarian, but Spanish, although it appeared that she had not known a word of that language before her illness. They had to engage a Spanish interpreter to translate to her bewildered Hungarian parents.

Chattering in voluble Spanish, the fifteen-year-old girl declared that she was Señora Lucia Altarex de Salvio, wife of a working man in Madrid. She said she had fourteen children, and was forty years old. She sang Spanish songs, and preferred Spanish food. She became fond of her parents, but insisted that she couldn't understand why they should pretend to be her father and mother. She was homesick for her supposed family in Madrid, and couldn't guess how she ever got to Budapest.

"I was sick," she cried, "and I died, and now I have come back to live in this strange country, among strange people."

What was the explanation? Transmigration? The transmigration of a soul? Or was it some weird turn of mere mental disturbance? Prominent psychiatrists studied the girl, trying to find out. The climax of the investigation came when they brought her before a committee composed of eminent medical men. The chief of police of Budapest and the Spanish minister were also present. They gave her a thorough questioning, discovered that she spoke rather poor Spanish. She used expressions that showed she wasn't a native of Spain at all. While all this was going on, the Budapest cops searched her house, and found in a cupboard Spanish dictionaries, Spanish grammars, Spanish textbooks. The young Hungarian turned out to be a pathological liar of a most complicated sort.

IN A TOWN IN ITALY, A NUN LAY IN HER CONVENT CELL, and her forehead streamed with blood. The pious folk of those parts were not astonished, for it was Good Friday. Every Good Friday, for sixteen years, a sign of wonder

had come to Sister Elena Aiello, a nun in a convent or-
phanage at the City of Cosenza, southern Italy. She would
take to her bed, pass into a trance of religious ecstasy, and
from her forehead blood would ooze and stream. To the
local people it was a miraculous stigmatum—a sign of the
Crown of Thorns which was pressed upon the brow of the
Saviour.

Such was the story of the miracle every Good Friday
for sixteen years. When it occurred again in 1940 physicians studied the prodigy. They reported that blood indeed did issue from the nun's forehead, staining the pillows.
They said she did not appear to suffer. She lay in a trance
with a faint smile on her lips. The doctors suggested no
explanation of the phenomenon regarded as a Good Friday miracle by scores of believers, who knelt and prayed
outside of the convent cell.

IN NEW YORK, SALVATORE MORRIONE WAS TIRED OF IT ALL
and decided to end it. He went down into the basement of
the building where he lived, put a pistol to his head and
pulled the trigger. The shot rang out, but Morrione didn't
feel anything. He thought that was odd, and pulled the
trigger again: the same thing happened. He examined the
gun to see what was wrong. Nothing, apparently. So for
the third time he put the pistol to his head, and fired. Once

more he heard the shot but didn't feel a thing. He threw away the gun in disgust and walked up the stairs to his second-floor flat. There his family saw that he was bleeding and called an ambulance.

The hospital report showed that all three bullets penetrated Morrione's skull and brain. One was lodged at the base of the brain, the other two, back of the right eye. Hemorrhage, concussion and a fracture of the skull. Morrione kept on insisting to the doctors that he felt nothing. The amazed surgeons performed a complicated operation. The patient eventually died.

LIMA, PERU, REPORTED AN EXTRAORDINARY EVENT. A BEAUtiful young woman was walking along the street when lightning hit her, ripped off all her clothes and deprived her of the power of speech. Near by was a man who had long been mute. When he saw the nude young lady, his power of speech was immediately restored to him. We would like to know the first thing said by the man who had long been mute.

A weird one from Italy. A man named Acerbo went crazy. A neighbor named Brugna took him in his car to convey him to a lunatic asylum. As they drove along, the car collided with a truck. Both the insane Acerbo and his custodian Brugna were injured. They were taken to a hospital, and there the doctors discovered that as a result of the crash Acerbo had become sane and Brugna had gone crazy.

Here's something that sounds like a joke, but it's a tragedy. It happened in Spain, where almost anything fantastic can occur. In Barcelona a truck was rolling along carrying an empty coffin. A farmer who was hitch-hiking thumbed a ride. He was bouncing along in the rear of the truck, which was open, when it started to rain. He examined the coffin, found it empty, and crawled inside to keep dry. There he fell asleep.

Further on, two other hitch-hikers got a ride on the truck. They were going along at a lively clip when the farmer inside the coffin pushed open the lid, stuck his head out and observed: "Oh, it has stopped raining." The two other hitch-hikers were so terrified that they leaped from the speeding truck. One was killed.

AT KINGSTON, ONTARIO, DELBERT BRADLEY OWED HIS LIFE to the way the horn of his automobile smacked when the crash came. Early in the morning, in an isolated section, his car got out of control, went off the road, and crashed into a culvert. Delbert was knocked unconscious and badly cut, so seriously that he would have bled to death had it not been for what had happened to the automobile horn. It was jammed in such fashion that the electrical control was grounded, and this made the horn blast away. It kept on blowing. It echoed across hill and dale. The pestilential noise awakened farmers, annoyed them. Finally they went to take a look and see what was causing that incessant horn-blowing. So they discovered the crash, and saved a life.

AT FRAMINGHAM, MASSACHUSETTS, THERE'S A WOMAN'S reformatory. Three of its young inmates escaped. They wanted to get as far away as possible, but had no money and no car. So they started to pursue their travels by thumbing. After several cars had passed them, one driver stopped, and the girls got a free ride. It was a police car, looking for them!

HARRY OLSON OF CHICAGO HAD HIS AUTOMOBILE STOLEN, and turned hitch-hiker to get a ride home. He was picked up by his own car, in which was the man who had stolen it.

*
=

PRINCE EDWARD ISLAND, IN THE GULF OF ST. LAWRENCE, reported the strange news of Charles Coughlin's homecoming. He was a native of the island who in eighteen ninety-five started traveling and a few years later wound up at Galveston, Texas. He died there, and was buried. On September eighth, nineteen hundred and one, a terrific West Indian hurricane swept the Gulf of Mexico, and caused that historic calamity of the Southwest known as the Galveston flood. The wind blasted at a terrific velocity of a hundred and thirty-five miles an hour, and swept the raging waters over the city. The churning torrents washed out the cemetery where Charles Coughlin was buried. The water swept away the earth and the coffins, which floated out on the Gulf.

Thirty-four years later, in nineteen thirty-five, a floating coffin drifted ashore at Prince Edward Island. Upon examination, they found a plate with the name of Charles Coughlin, the same man who had left his Prince Edward Island home those long years ago. Wind and current had carried the coffin from the Gulf of Mexico off Galveston for thousands of miles—all the way around into the Atlantic and up the coast to the Gulf of the St. Lawrence. An unusual way for a local boy to return home.

IN INDIA ONE OF THE STRANGEST OF COURT CASES WAS SET-tled—the final decision given. It was a lawsuit against Sri Sri Iswrai Bahudaneswai Thuk Urani. What's so strange about that—except the elaborate name? The defendant was a god, an idol. The suit was brought against a jewel-studded image that stood in a Hindu temple.

The testimony before the court told how years in the past there were two pious brothers who were greatly out of luck. They were desperately poor and couldn't seem to make a go of it. What did they do? They made an idol. With humble, patient hands they fashioned an image of divinity. They set it up and worshiped it—something like that "idol made of mud that they call the great God Bud." At once prospects improved for the two Hindu brothers. Their affairs flourished, and they became fabulously rich. For this they thanked the idol they had made, the divinity their hands had fashioned. They dowered it with jewels and built a glowing shrine for it, and great throngs came to worship. When they died, the brothers left their property to the idol, large possessions of lands and villages. The shrine of Sri Sri Iswrai Bahudaneswai Thuk Urani became more and more a center of religious enthusiasm.

[251]

The relatives of the two pious rich men went to court, claiming that they were the rightful heirs to the estate—not the idol made of mud. The case dragged for twenty years. The high court of Bengal gave a compromise verdict, decreeing that the divinity was entitled to only a portion of the land and income. Whereupon the idol appealed to the high court in London: its guardians did. Finally the high court closed the case by upholding the verdict. So Sri Sri Iswrai Bahudaneswai Thuk Urani got only a part of the estate of the pious brothers.

A TWENTIETH-CENTURY FRANKENSTEIN WAS THE VICTIM of a weird mishap. Remember our old friend Frankenstein, the man who created a monster which eventually turned upon him and tore him to pieces? His contemporary counterpart was an inventor who lived at Brighton, the Atlantic City or Asbury Park of England. He constructed a robot —a mechanical man which he christened Alpha. The remarkable automaton could do all sorts of astonishing things, and the inventor was giving a demonstration of these wonders to a crowd of spectators. Alpha told the time, read newspapers, answered questions, and could even handle firearms.

Alpha was ordered to fire a revolver. Whom do you suppose he shot? Yes, you guessed it. Alpha shot his master instead of the target. The wound was not as serious as the damage wrought on the Frankenstein of fiction by his monster, but it was enough to persuade the inventor that Alpha was no fit person to be trusted with a gun.

SILENCE WAS INDEED GOLDEN, SO FAR AS MRS. GEORGE Ward was concerned.

Mr. and Mrs. Ward were in a Chicago furniture store. Bandits entered and held up the place. They told Mr. and Mrs. Ward to sit down and remain quiet—not a peep. That command was obeyed, especially by Mrs. Ward. She didn't utter one syllable.

"I'm glad they didn't ask me to talk," she declared after the bandits had gone, "because when they held up the store I found a chance to slip my rings into my mouth, and if I had tried to say anything with that mouthful of rings it surely would have been awkward."

The rings were worth nearly a thousand dollars. So the silence was altogether golden.

MRS. BEULAH HOPKINS OF GARY, INDIANA, WAS IN THE bathroom having a bath. Her husband outside suddenly heard a scream. He dashed into the bathroom—no wife! The bewildered husband looked out of the window, and there was the little woman on top of a sand pile three stories below. The Missus had rather hurriedly slipped on something and dropped out in the street. That is, she slipped on a piece of soap, and tobogganed right out the bathroom window.

IN EIGHTEEN NINETY, A MAN IN A SLEIGH DROVE BY THE farm of Mrs. John R. McDonald—a nattily dressed man who wore a nifty black derby hat. A sudden gust of wind, and the derby went whirling through the air, on to Mrs. McDonald's property. The owner looked vainly for it, and at length drove on bareheaded. Mrs. McDonald retrieved the derby and for years the hat was worn by members of her family—until it wore out.

Forty-five years later Mrs. McDonald advertised for the owner of the hat. She wanted to return to him the long-since-worn-out derby. Because, she said: "It has been on my conscience ever since eighteen ninety." That after it had been for so long on the heads of members of her family!

THE BIGGEST WINE CASK IN THE WORLD WAS FALLING TO pieces. It was in Hungary, and it held twenty-five thousand eight hundred gallons of the juice of the grape—or it did before it began to sag and collapse. The cask belonged to Hungarians but was built by Englishmen—on a bet.

Away back in the last century a party of noble British sportsmen paid a visit to the broad acres of Count Esterhazy, the great Hungarian magnate. They told the Count they'd shoot every pheasant on his estate. Instead of being alarmed or angry, Esterhazy made them a bet—that they couldn't do it.

"If you succeed in shooting all my pheasants," he declared, "I'll have the birds made into one huge pheasant pie and sent to your London Club. But if you don't shoot them all, you'll have to build me a wine cask holding as many Hungarian measures of wine as birds that you shoot."

The Hungarian measure of wine was the equivalent of twelve gallons. The Englishmen lost the bet. They didn't shoot all the pheasants, but they did shoot more than two thousand. So, according to the terms of the bet, they had to provide Count Esterhazy with a cask holding twenty-five thousand eight hundred gallons of wine. They went back to England, and had it built and sent to Hungary.

The giant cask was filled to the top only three times. On the last occasion it was emptied at one sitting by a regiment of Austrian infantry. That's the way the story went. The regiment, having drunk the twenty-five thousand gallons, was out of commission for two days. I don't know if that wine-drinking exploit is possible, but if a regiment of World

War American doughboys had ever got to Hungary they'd have tried it.

But anyway the historic cask was falling apart and caving in, and by now it must be a wreck—if they haven't used it for firewood.

HERE'S THE MOST FREAKISH HOBBY I EVER HEARD OF. Imagine a man collecting the skins of tattooed people? He was Doctor Fukushi, a lecturer at the Tokyo Imperial University.

The Doctor scored a triumph when he discovered a fifty-seven-year-old barber who was entirely tattooed. Every square inch of that man's body bore some sort of ornamental design, except his face. As soon as the Doctor heard of this curiosity he rushed to see the man and obtained the barber's promise to bequeath him his skin.

Doctor Fukushi had been collecting tattooed skins for twenty-six years. He had in his possession some mighty choice specimens, and no less than eighteen people had promised to bequeath their epidermis to him in their wills.

IN A BROOKLYN COURT A MIDGET MADE A COMPLAINT THAT a side-show owner wanted him to act as a barker—take his place outside and ballyhoo the show.

Said the midget to the judge: "I wouldn't be a barker! It would make me look like a freak!"

Comic Conclusion

SOME stories of this human life of ours are simply comic. They come under the heading of a laugh—and nothing more. We find the happening that's a sheer absurdity and the solemn affair with a kicker on the end. The merry mix-ups of mankind, the Pageant of Life at its funniest.

AT KENNET SQUARE, PENNSYLVANIA, MRS. EVA SHUBER wanted to surprise her husband. She had never driven a car, so she knew how it would astonish him if she were to jump in the family bus and drive off with a smart exhibition at the wheel. So she thought she'd have some practice.

Mrs. Shuber started the car going, and tried to turn

[258]

around. She drove it for a wild plunge across a lawn, and crashed into the corner of her grandmother's house. Then she backed the car, and cut another swath across the lawn and knocked down the water pump in the front yard. She started forward again, and this time went mowing through the flower beds and struck another corner of her grandmother's house. She backed once more and this time hit a wash boiler, which bounced up and banged the car. Then she hit grandma's house a third time. The car glanced off and bounced against a tree, and there it stayed, immovably wedged between the house and the tree. By this time the police arrived, and of course found that Mrs. Shuber had no license.

P.S. Was her husband surprised? Yes!

BATTLING ZUNIGA AND TONY SANTOS MIXED IT IN LIVELY fashion for three rounds. At the end of the third Santos went to his corner and sat down, slumping the way boxers do between rounds. One of his seconds was the excitable sort. The thrill of battle had him wildly excited. He reached for the water bottle to give the weary boxer a drink. But instead of the water bottle he got hold of a flask containing smelling salts. He held it up to the boxer's lips, and the thirsty fighting man took a long, long swallow.

Smelling salts, as we all know, consist largely of ammonia,

and a long drink of ammonia is a powerful refreshment. The unfortunate boxer just about turned a couple of somersaults. When the bell for the fourth round clanged he was still somersaulting. The referee called the bout off, and awarded the fight to Battling Zuniga. He won by what might be termed a medicated knockout.

W. Augustus Shipley, formerly an alderman of Queens County, New York, had a pair of handcuffs presented to him by the sheriff of the county. This pair of manacles was famous for having been used in one of the big sensational criminal cases. The ex-alderman was showing them to a friend, and the friend said: "Try 'em, Gus, and see how they look on you." So Gus tried them on. He snapped the handcuffs on his wrist, and then remembered that his friend the sheriff had never given him the keys for them. He couldn't get them off.

The handcuffs were strong and stanch in every respect. Ex-alderman Gus called in all kinds of assistance, from carpenters to locksmiths. It was not until five hours later that an expert was able to open the lock and remove the historic handcuffs from the wrists of the former alderman of Queens.

*

Mastro Stefano, a seventy-year-old mill worker, was excessively proud of his mustache, a huge pair of handle bars. He went into a barber shop, was snoozing in the chair, and the barber cut off the famous mustache. Mastro Stefano sued the barber for two thousand dollars damages. He told the court that it was a beautiful mustache, and that it had taken him forty-seven years to grow and train it.

The barber said: "It looked like walrus whiskers. I thought I was doing the community a favor."

The court awarded Mastro Stefano twenty-five dollars damages on the ground that he'd been the victim of "technical tresspass on the face."

At Seattle, Washington, Mrs. D. D. Ringer made a big mistake—or was it Mr. Ringer who made a mistake? Upon returning home from a bridge party, Mrs. Ringer walked into the bedroom and saw a man asleep on the bed. She ran out of the house and called the police, saying that a strange man was sleeping in the house and that he must be a burglar. The police arrived and laid violent hands on the man sleeping on the bed. The man jumped up roaring with indignation:

"What's the idea? Can't a man take a nap in his own home?"

Then Mrs. Ringer recognized him. He was Mr. Ringer,

who had just been to a barber shop and had his mustache shaved off. Its absence had left Mr. Ringer unrecognizable even to his own wife.

*
=

CHUJI KOSUMI WAS A JAPANESE WHO DIDN'T LIKE TO BE fooled. Chuji Kosumi had arrived in New York from Japan, and maybe out in the Far East he had heard about the ways of the big city. He was on the lookout. No smart New Yorker was going to take him into camp as a greenhorn Far Eastern Reuben come to town.

Having a bit of an appetite and being curious about American food, he walked into a Third Avenue doughnut shop and ordered some crullers. Chuji Kosumi looked at the sinkers with a skeptical eye. They had holes in them.

"Honorable Sir," he said to the proprietor, "because I am Japanese you think you can cheat me. You sell me some sinkers, but you sell me some hole in the middle. But you no cheat Chuji Kosumi."

The cruller magnate thought he was being kidded. So he replied that if Chuji Kosumi didn't like the holes in the sinkers he could order up some fried scallops and plug up the holes.

The man from Nippon was insulted. He reached for a custard pie. He must have seen pie-throwing American movies back in Tokyo or Osaka. The pie hit the proprietor. Chuji Kosumi reached for a lemon meringue pie, then a chocolate pie. The proprietor was covered with humiliation and pie. Chuji Kosumi followed through with the mustard pot and the ketchup bottle.

Presently Chuji Kosumi was in jail. In solitude there he had a chance to look up the subject of sinkers. He learned that it was natural for the doughnuts to have holes in the middle. He said he was sorry. Excuse please.

HERE'S A STORY WITH A LOT OF PEP—I MEAN REAL PEPPER. A girl went into a Chinese restaurant in Chicago and told Wing Foo Sam, a waiter, that she wanted an order of chow mein to take out. She said she wanted a first-class order because, as she explained, "It's for a mighty nice chap." Wing Foo Sam brought the chow mein, the girl took it away, and a few minutes later the trouble began. There was one roaring protest from the fellow who ate the chow mein. It nearly burnt his face off. He thought he was eating liquid fire.

When the complaint came blazing back to the restaurant, Wing Foo Sam was instantly fired by his Chinese boss. But when Wing Foo explained the matter, he got his job right back. It appears that when the girl said the chow mein was for a mighty nice chap, Wing Foo Sam misunderstood her. He thought she said it was for a mighty nice Jap. His Chinese patriotic blood arose in him, and he heard the voices of his ancestors. So Wing Foo Sam decided he'd fix that mighty nice Jap up good and proper. He spiced the chow mein with three teaspoonfuls of blazing red pepper.

AT THE UNIVERSITY OF MICHIGAN, PRESIDENT ALEXANDER Ruthven entertained a party of students at tea. One was a Chinese, recently arrived. He had been memorizing appropriate English expressions from a book of English and Chinese phrases. In preparation for the university president's tea party, he looked up the right thing to say and committed it to memory word for word. So when the college prexy handed him a cup of tea, he responded with the utmost politeness,

"Thank you, sir or madam, as the case may be." Straight from the phrase book.

WE ALL MAKE SLIPS OF ENGLISH. I KNOW I DO, THOUGH when you talk on the radio you're supposed to be mighty careful about the correct use of words. Sometimes all that correctness is a bit oppressive, and you feel like letting go, toss grammar and syntax to the winds, and break all the rules. So it was a pleasure one night to reel off a line of astonishing English. A dispatch from Newark told of a letter sent to the Alcohol Commissioner's office, a letter of complaint from a man who lived above a tavern:

"I am living myself over the saloon and one more family living here. One time family moving out because it is horrible, too much noise, late almost every nights. Also too many young womens yelling all nights. All I want is more reasonable and much more quieter that we could stay in our house and having little of sleeping in nights."

THAT ONE BROUGHT A RESPONSE—FROM BRAZIL OF ALL places. J. E. Millender, vice-president of an electric light company at Porto Alegro, sent me a remarkable specimen of English to match it. It was a letter written by a local Brazilian in English—a complaint because the electricity had not been installed.

"Dear Mr. Millender: Hoping to your permission, I have to start a question and to importune you on account of the electric light. My lovely wife is waiting for the light. I have bought her one of your electric smoothing iron—and now she wishes to smooth. Dear Sir—have you ever heard once the sing-song of wives when the whole day is stormy? If yes, then you have a cognizance of the quarrelsomeness what my wife has to me because she has the wires, electric lamps and smoothing iron in the house, and she cannot use them. And now the matter is this—if you are unmarried, you should be forced to marry my good wife, then I should be convinced that you would immediately order all your workmen to my street for put posts and wires."

A LETTER ADDRESSED TO MR. JOHN MILTON, AUTHOR OF *Paradise Lost*, was received at Columbia University. The university authorities had considerable difficulty in delivering the letter, because Mr. Milton died in 1674, and has not been seen since.

Investigation showed that the letter had been written by a young salesman employed in a press clipping bureau. He had learned that the Columbia University Press was bringing out a new edition of Milton's poems. Along with that information he found that some of Mr. Milton's work was well thought of. So he wrote to ask if Mr. Milton would not like to subscribe to his clipping service, so that he might see how his poetry was received in the American press.

AT FORT SLOCUM, NEW YORK, PRIVATE SOLOMON OF Brooklyn was being questioned by the sergeant. The top kick asked: "Private Solomon, what's your first name?"

"Solomon," replied Solomon.

"Oh, a wise guy," barked the top kick. "What's your middle name?"

"Solomon," replied Solomon.

"Say, listen, wise guy . . ." the sergeant was exploding.

The rookie was dead serious about it all. His full name was Solomon Solomon Solomon. He should have been a wise guy indeed—with three times the wisdom of Solomon.

IN CHICAGO A MAN WENT TO COURT TO HAVE HIS NAME changed. He was a merchant, and said his name was such that his customers couldn't remember it, couldn't pronounce it, got it all balled up. What was the name? Harris. Louis Harris petitioned to have his name changed to Haralampopoulas. Which certainly did sound like the old story of man bites dog.

The answer to the paradox was that the merchant's customers were Greeks, and they found Harris an exceedingly difficult name to remember and pronounce. Amazing, the way they got all tangled up in trying to say—Harris. But as for Haralampopoulas, they rattled it off with fluent ease. So presently the customers were saying, "Okay, Haralampopoulas; we sure are glad you got rid of that outlandish jawbreaker of a name you used to have!"

Mills Thompson, former art editor of the *Saturday Evening Post*, had the cellar of his house cleaned by an old Negro. When the job was done, the colored man said: "Boss, I'se got your cellar clean as a whistle, and it's two dollars, and I hopes if you has any more work like dat, I gits it."

"I don't see why not," responded Mr. Thompson. "What's your name?"

"George Washington, sah."

"Seems to me I've heard that name before."

"I guess you has, boss. I been takin' out ashes round here for years."

In Mississippi a colored gentleman was on trial charged with murder. The evidence was all in, and the jury was deliberating its verdict. After the jurors had been out for an hour, the defendant became nervous and impatient. He stood up and said to the court:

"Judge, guess I'll plead guilty to manslaughter."

The judge accepted the plea and sentenced the man to seven and a half years in prison. Just as he had passed the sentence, the jury came back into court.

"What is your verdict, gentlemen?" demanded the judge.

"*Not* guilty," said the foreman.

But the judge's sentence stood. Seven and a half years for talking out of turn.

AT GRAND RAPIDS, MICHIGAN, A COLORED GENTLEMAN WAS arrested on a charge of driving a car while intoxicated. When he came up for trial the police surgeon testified that in his opinion the charge was true. The magistrate asked why. The surgeon replied that he had noted that the pupils of the prisoner's eyes were dilated.

The court then spoke to the prisoner about the dilation of his eyes.

The prisoner replied: "I dunno, Yo' Honah. But here, you-all look for yourself."

So saying, he took out his glass eye, and handed it to the judge. The prisoner was discharged.

AT GREENBURGH, NEW YORK, JAMES EDWARD WILLIAMS was a black man and a large man, a Negro tall, broad-shouldered and brawny. James Edward Williams was also a man with a thirst, a man of capacity, who took his drinks and plenty of them. He was on trial for illegal manufacture of liquor. He had operated an illicit still that had turned out vast quantities of fire water. His defense was that he didn't make the hootch commercially to sell it. That would be against the law. He was manufacturing hundreds of gallons of whiskey just for his own consumption.

The judge exclaimed in amazement: "A hundred-gallon still for your own use?"

The prosecuting attorney added: "And there were sixteen hundred gallons of mash up there?"

Whereupon James Edward Williams came up with this reply: "Well, that's not much."

"And this is not much," retorted the judge. "Six months in jail!"

THE CHAMPION DRINKER OF BULGARIA DIED, AND HE DIDN'T drink himself to death. Gorgioff Sando was acclaimed the most copious toper of the Bulgars, and you can sing all the drinking songs you know to his memory, from "Nut Brown Ale," to "Maine Stein Song." He drank everything from beer to vodka, and never touched water until he died.

On the day of his death Gorgioff Sando downed fifty-one bottles of red wine in the village tavern. Did that kill him? No, not at all. He called for more, but the tavern keeper said it was too late, and he wanted to close up. So Gorgioff Sando went home and down the stairs to his cellar, where he kept his wine casks. He had a nightcap of a quart or two. But it was water that killed him.

There was a sudden torrential downpour, a flooded stream, a rush of water into the cellar. The Bulgarians said that at the first touch of water Gorgioff Sando died. He never could stand water. They found him the next morning in the flood-filled cellar. He was a gentleman and a scholar, but no judge of water.

A SOVIET OFFICIAL TOLD OF MEETING TWO AMERICAN MIL-lionaires in Paris who had been on a trip to Russia and were most enthusiastic. They were decidedly musical, and expressed great admiration for those beautiful Russian folk songs. They told of two delightful chaps they had met in Russia who had taught them many of the lovely songs. They had also played poker quite a bit. While the games were going on, the Russians used to sing in a dreamy, old-fashioned way. The Americans had learned the folk songs —memorizing the tunes and even the Russian words. They added that they had lost five thousand dollars or so in the poker games, but that the songs they had learned were so beautiful they didn't mind.

When the two Americans told this story, the Soviet official asked them to sing the songs. The Americans did, chanting the Russian words. That's when the Soviet official began to laugh. The quaint Russian words sung to the beautiful tunes were something like this:—

"I have two pair—Queens and Jacks."

"Well, I have three Aces. Let's keep on raising."

No wonder that the two American millionaires learned plenty of Russian folk songs and lost five thousand dollars.

A MISHAP IN CHICAGO WAS ALONG THE LINE OF THE OLD story of the chicken thief—the one telling how a farmer heard someone in his hen house one night, and shouted: "Who's there? Better answer quick or I'll shoot." Whereupon a voice came from the chicken coop saying plaintively: "There ain't nobody here but us chickens."

In the Chicago incident a burglar broke into a tailor's place. Moving clumsily, he stubbed his toe, and made a noise. The tailor's wife called out: "Now Tommy, Tommy, get back into your box."

Thereupon the burglar lifted up his voice and said: "Meow, meow!" He always was good at imitating a cat.

It was a mistake, however. What he should have said was "Bow, wow!" Because Tommy was not a cat but a wire-haired fox terrier. All Toms are not cats, as the burglar had leisure to reflect sadly in a jail cell.

E. F. Hutton of New York was a broker and philan-thropist. In a little New York church he established a place to distribute food to the needy. He financed it with fifty thousand dollars.

One day E. F. Hutton paid a visit to that little charitable institution of his. He went in a taxi and, not wanting to be conspicuous, got out of the taxi a short distance down the street. Then he walked quietly into the church where the food was being passed out.

The taxi driver watched him and then came running after him into the church. The taxi driver thought he was doing something noble. He hollered to the man in charge of the food distribution: "Hey, don't give this guy anything." Then he pointed an accusing finger. "Why, he came here in a taxi. He's got money."

Doctor Engel of New York, a pioneer of the Holly-wood diet of pineapple and lamb chops, told this one: A fat lady went to a diet specialist, and was instructed: "Eat pine-apple and lamb chops twice a day." She promised faithfully that she would.

A month later she came back, and she had put on about ten more pounds. The doctor said, "Did you do as I told you, and eat pineapple and lamb chops twice a day?"

"I did, doctor," she vowed.

"Did you eat anything else?" he demanded suspiciously.
"Nothing," she replied, "except my regular meals."

IMAGINE A SWAGGER CAFÉ IN THE ETERNAL CITY. A WELL-dressed Roman of proud and distinguished bearing stalks to the bar and orders vermouth. Italian vermouth, not French —because patriotic Italians refuse to buy anything produced by the sanctionist countries boycotting Italy. Suddenly he notices that the bartender is serving another customer with a drink of Scotch whisky.

The occurrence was described in a letter I received from Bill Courtney, war correspondent for *Collier's*. Bill described how that Roman patriot flared up when he saw that bottle of Scotch. "Don't you know," he shouted at the bartender, "that's British whisky? And Great Britain is the ringleader of the sanctionists?" On he stormed in blazing Italian, shouting that no patriotic Italian bartender would serve Scotch.

He got so excited that his hat fell off. The unfortunate bartender, timid and trembling after this nationalistic bawling out, was eager to pacify the angry patriot. He rushed around the bar, and with frightened politeness hastened to pick up the gentleman's hat. He was dusting it off obsequiously when he noticed the label in the lining. It was a London hat, made by a fashionable firm of British hatters.

[274]

Whereupon the bartender's courage returned. He glared sternly at the customer. "Your hat was made in England," he cried accusingly.

It was the customer's turn to be embarrassed. "But," he stammered with apologies, "it's an old hat."

"And this," replied the bartender with dignity, "is an old whisky."

DOWN UNDER, IN THE SOUTHERN CONTINENT OF AUSTRALIA, court was in session. The judge was on the bench in all his dignity. A learned array of lawyers was there. The court-room was crowded, because it was a sensational case. A man was suing his uncle for alienation of affections. He claimed that his uncle stole his wife's love. That kind of lawsuit attracts a lot of attention anywhere in the world, and it was one of the local sensations in Australia.

The testimony was about to begin when the defendant, the love-pirate uncle, arose and pointed at the jury. "Look," he shouted, "look!"

That was when the judge's eyes grew wide. He gasped, and his dignified British judicial wig nearly fell off his head. Consternation reigned in the courtroom—because, there among the jurymen, ready to try the case, was the plaintiff. He was sitting on the jury that was to give a decision in his own lawsuit.

There had been a slight mix-up when the jury had been

[275]

selected. The name of the plaintiff had accidentally been included among those of the jurors called to serve, and the chap didn't seem to mind it at all. He went right through the proceedings, ready to render a decision—presumably in favor of himself. The slip wasn't noticed until the jury filed in and the love-pirate uncle saw his nephew, big and bold, among the twelve men good and true. Whereupon the nephew did the Australian crawl out of the jury box, and British courtroom dignity was resumed.

IN WEST VIRGINIA CHARLIE CLARK WAS A HUMORIST. HE loved jokes. Charlie was in the county jail, and played pranks on the guards. One of his tricks was to stuff wire and pieces of wood into the locks on the cells so they couldn't get the prisoners out. They had to send for a locksmith, and it took three hours before the cell doors could be opened. Finally Charlie's fellow prisoners couldn't stand his jokes any longer. They raised a fund to hire a lawyer and get the humorist out of jail.

FROM CHINA CAME THE STORY OF THE MERRY DOOM OF Li Feng-Yin—he died laughing. We've all used the expression, "thought I'd die laughing." Li Feng-Yin did. Not that he was such an enormously jolly fellow, whose life was given over to chuckles, Chinese jokes and the Far Eastern merry ha-ha. Li Feng-Yin was a kidnaper. The Peiping police got after him and caught him. But Li didn't die laughing over that. He was brought before the Celestial judge, who sentenced him to death. He didn't die laughing at that either. He was condemned to be shot, instead of being decapitated in the more characteristic Chinese way. Neither did that cause Li to die laughing.

The story was this—that his case was appealed and his death sentence was commuted to fifteen years in the penitentiary. That was the cause for laughter, and Li decided to celebrate merrily with his fellow prisoners. They bribed the jailors and got stacks of food and drink—plenty of bird's-nest soup and rice wine. They dined and wined and drank to Li's escape from the executioners. With every toast, Li Feng-Yin laughed louder and louder, until finally he fell over, having laughed himself to death.

Now we come to a really ticklish subject—boredom. You know how it is when somebody talks on and on, and you're bored. Maybe it's a political speech, maybe it's a sermon in church, maybe it's a lecture on sociology, maybe it's a would-be facetious after-dinner speech, or maybe it's somebody on the radio talking about the news of the day. From the British House of Lords we learned that even dukes could be boring. A marquis could windily weary you to death. In fact, a Britisher would tell you that anybody can be a bore, except His Majesty, the King.

In the House of Peers, Lord Kilmaine arose and presented a resolution against long speeches. He pointed out that extended preambles, delayed climaxes and eternal perorations are so long-drawn-out in the House of Peers that their lordships had found a clever way to dodge the oratory. They sneaked out into the library and read *Punch*, until somebody punched a bell signaling that the speaker had stopped. Then they adjusted their eyeglasses and returned.

Lord Kilmaine went on to explain why girls leave home, likewise boys, also why husbands leave wives and wives leave husbands. Also why people tune out a speaker on the radio. Because they're bored. His Lordship then made a ringing declaration: "I have listened," he proclaimed, "to sermons so long that their only effect was to make me want to go out and break all the Ten Commandments, one right after the other." Then he said some more about long speeches, contributed some further comment about how wearisome they were, and indulged in some additional reflections about boredom.

At this point another noble Peer interrupted and pointed to a whole string of lords on their way to the library, thereby proving that a speech about boredom could be an awful bore.

[278]